THE
FALL AND RISE
OF THE
ASIATIC MODE
OF
PRODUCTION

THE
FALL AND RISE
OF THE
ASIATIC MODE
OF
PRODUCTION

Stephen P. Dunn

Routledge & Kegan Paul
London, Boston, Melbourne and Henley

First published in 1982
by Routledge & Kegan Paul Ltd
39 Store Street, London WC1E 7DD,
9 Park Street, Boston, Mass. 02108, USA,
296 Beaconsfield Parade, Middle Park,
Melbourne, 3206, Australia and
Broadway House, Newtown Road,
Henley-on-Thames, Oxon. RG9 1EN
Set in 11 on 13 pt VIP Times by
Inforum Ltd, Portsmouth
and printed in Great Britain by
Hartnoll Print, Bodmin, Cornwall

Library of Congress Cataloging in Publication Data

Dunn, Stephen Porter, 1928–
The fall and rise of the Asiatic mode of
production.
1. Asiatic mode of production.   I. Title.
HB97.5.D845   335.4'12   82—5222
ISBN 0 7100 9053 6   AACR2

Felix qui potuit rerum cognoscere causas.

Vergil, *Georgics*

Die Philosophen haben bisher nur die Welt in verschiedene Weisen interpretiert. Es geht nun darauf hin, sie zu verändern.

Karl Marx, *Thesen Über Feuerbach*

CONTENTS

Preface *viii*

Part one: Decline and fall *1*

Introduction *3*
Decline and fall: 1929–34 *7*

Part two: Resurgence *39*

Interregnum: 1934–64 *42*
Prelude to the partial revival of the Asiatic mode of
production: *ca* 1948–64 *63*
The revival of the Asiatic mode of production *77*
Epilogue: 1975– *121*
Conclusions *122*

Notes *125*

PREFACE

Marx and Engels themselves can never be taken simply at their word: the errors of their writings on the past should not be evaded or ignored, but identified and criticized. To do so is not to depart from historical materialism, but to rejoin it. There is no place for any fideism in rational knowledge, which is necessarily cumulative; and the greatness of the founders of new sciences has never been proof against misjudgments or myths, any more than it has been impaired by them. To take 'liberties' with the signature of Marx is in this sense merely to enter into the freedom of Marxism. (Perry Anderson, *Passages from Antiquity to Feudalism*, London, NLB Press, 1974, p. 9)

This book, although not particularly long, has been an unconscionable time in the writing. Some of the delay can be blamed on force of circumstance, and some on the difficulty of the topic, but when all allowances have been made, there is a remainder for which only the author's dilatory habits can be held responsible.

The original seed of this work was laid down in the fall of 1965, when the selected materials of the debate between V.V. Struve and the French scholars Maurice Godelier and Jean Suret-Canale, published in *Narody Azii i Afriki*, came to my attention. I did not then realize the magnitude of the task which I would be undertaking, but it was immediately obvious that an important change in the Marxist theory of history was in progress or was about to take place.

In 1970, I received a grant from the American Council of Learned Societies under the general title 'Soviet Studies on the Ancient Eastern State.' The initial results of this work were presented in a paper read before the Far Western Slavic Conference at Portland, Oregon, in the spring of 1972; that paper was essentially an outline version of part one of the present work. Since that time, I have had to do the research and writing necessary to complete the task in the intervals of other work – not to speak of having to wait, at times, for new materials from the Soviet Union which would answer some of the outstanding questions. The reader will soon see that by no means all of the questions have yet been answered.

I wish here to thank publicly all those who have been involved in this project – either by choice or merely by having had it repeatedly thrust under their noses. In particular, my thanks are due to my wife, Ethel, for her support and her editorial assistance in the final stages of preparation – both of them given, I may add, in the face of a certain lack of interest in the subject-matter; to my friend William M. Mandel, who, since I arrived in Berkeley in the fall of 1963, has been my mentor in formal Marxism and in the history of the socialist movement, for his painstaking critical reading of the text and his very valuable suggestions; and to another friend, Dr Albert R. Vogeler (currently at the Department of History, California State College at Fullerton), for a general critique from the point of view of a professional historian. Here I should also thank Professor Igor M. D'iakonov, Institute of Oriental Studies, Academy of Sciences, USSR (Leningrad Branch), who commented on my text and answered my questions with great candor and urbanity; and Professor Jan Pečirka

Preface

Caroline University, Prague, whose timely assistance in locating an obscure text is acknowledged at an appropriate point in the monograph.

In one sense, the sole aim of this monograph is to provide an account – as straightforward and complete as possible, with only a few departures from strict chronological sequence – of certain developments in Soviet intellectual history, along with the necessary auxiliary information to enable the reader to understand the issues involved. In this sense my work should be self-sufficient and self-explanatory. However, in another sense – the one which becomes relevant when we ask why anyone should bother to read what has been written here – this is a study not only in intellectual history, but in the theory of history itself, and one which raises important philosophical and methodological points. In this sense, it is imperative that the author states plainly his intellectual position and assumptions.

My own position throughout this work is that of an independent Marxist thinker and an equally independent political Marxist, which is to say that I regard myself as working within the Marxist intellectual and political traditions, broadly defined, but holding no particular allegiance to any of its existing subdivisions, and no fixed positions on the issues which currently divide the movement whose ideology is Marxism in the same broad sense. Furthermore, and quite apart from my own, or anyone else's, political position, I find it inconceivable that the activities and achievements of human beings, and ultimately the forms taken by human society, should not be subject to laws fundamentally analogous to those which govern the phenomena of the physical world. To put this another way: I am a theoretical Marxist because, and only because, Marxism is the only intellectual tradition which to my knowledge has made a forthright attempt to grasp the nettle represented by the assumed dichotomy in cognitive status between man and the physical world.

It will be clear from this that my position differs vastly from that commonly taken by social scientists of the school of thought currently prevailing in established academic circles in the USA and in part in Western Europe as well. While the place of Marxist methods and concepts in current Western academic social science, and the character of opposition to them in this context, are far beyond the scope of this work, I can refer the reader, purely for illustrative purposes, to a debate on the exploitation of peasants, participated in by George Dalton and others, including myself.[1] It is to be observed that the issues involved here – in this case, specifically that of the general validity of Marxist concepts such as 'exploitation,' and the classification of people according to their relationship to the means of production – are quite different from those raised by criticisms of specifically *Soviet* doctrine and practice from particular political and philosophical standpoints, including explicitly Marxist ones. These two types of issues are often unjustifiably confused, as a result of which the general validity of Marxist methods and concepts is portrayed as dependent on the nature and results of particular Soviet practices. Two especially glaring examples of this came to my attention recently.[2] In both of these cases, what the authors take to be the generally poor record of Soviet agriculture is turned into a general argument against the Marxist historical and economic theory as a whole, on the basis of an *a priori* assumption concerning the nature of man.[3] Furthermore, this assumption can be quite easily refuted from the ethnographic evidence relating to peoples at precapitalist stages of development; and the line of reasoning which connects the relative failures of Soviet agriculture (when judged by some unspecified standard) with the alleged lack of incentive on the part of Soviet agricultural workers can be laid to rest by comparing the results of Soviet with those of highly mechanized American industrial agriculture, where similar conditions (at least with regard to worker incentive) apparently prevail.

I have cited these two current examples (and they could be multiplied *ad infinitum*, if anyone willing to undertake such a melancholy task could be found) in order to indicate to the reader that the issues addressed in my main text are not as recondite or scholastic as they may appear at first glance. The central issue – and the one on which the reader should concentrate firmly, whatever may be the antics of the intellectual shuttlecock in tne debates to be summarized below – is precisely that of whether the historical process is to be regarded as single or double or multiple, as determined by one force, or by two related forces, or by a congeries of unspecifiable factors. It goes without saying that each of these alternative views has highly significant implications, both philosophically and in the narrow field of social science methodology. It is likewise noteworthy that the Western social scientists who are critical of Marxist methods on various grounds, do not, as far as I am aware, propose alternative theories of comparable breadth, but deny the validity of all 'single-factor explanations,' such as they (not altogether accurately) consider Marxism to be. This nihilistic approach on the part of those who would logically be its rivals places the Marxist intellectual tradition in a unique position, and gives the study of it an importance, and an interest, which go far beyond the bounds of academic intellectual history. If the development of the Marxist intellectual tradition (at least in its Soviet version) can be shown to be a scholastic phenomenon, an example of 'ideology' in the traditional and strict Marxist sense – that is to say, an *ex post facto* justification for particular interests – then one conclusion is appropriate, and that conclusion might be drawn from part one of the following text, *if it stood alone*. If, on the other hand, the Marxist intellectual tradition emerges from our investigation as a viable body of theory – like, for example,

Darwinian evolutionism – which is perhaps not provable *in toto*, but is nevertheless capable of developing out of its own resources, of accommodating new data, and of generating fresh insights, then a quite different conclusion is called for. I think the reader will see from the general tenor of part two that I favour the second view. Accordingly, whatever criticisms I may make – in terms of internal consistency or consistency with known historical facts – of particular applications of Marxist methods and their results, these criticisms will not be made from an implicitly or explicitly nihilistic or destructive point of view. My aim in whatever I have written on this topic has been rather to sharpen and refine the tools of Marxist analysis, to free them from accidental historical accretions and limitations of all types, and make them more powerful and less susceptible either to misuse for transient and secondary political purposes, or to hasty and ill-informed dismissal on the grounds of crude economic determinism or unavoidable political bias in their application and results.

A few words remain to be said as to the limitations of this work. I have dealt only with the Soviet literature on the topics under discussion, and have restricted my handling of the sources in English and other Western European languages to those dealing directly with issues of Soviet historiography. The grounds of this limitation are in part purely practical (my lack, in some cases, of the necessary linguistic equipment, and my desire to see the work, already too long delayed, in print within a reasonable time), but in part also intellectual. This work was originally planned as one section of a much larger book dealing with the development of Marxist intellectual tradition as it applied to the precapitalist social orders generally. When my work on the portion of this project published in the present volume was virtually complete, a book came to my attention which gives, in my opinion, an entirely adequate account of the portions of the topic which can be investi-

gated from non-Russian sources.[4] I have therefore decided
to regard the present volume as complete in itself, and to
proceed to other urgent matters. During the late stages of
my work, or after its completion, certain other materials
dealing with tangential aspects of the topic were published:[5] I decided to ignore these and to limit my treatment
to the Soviet Marxist intellectual tradition proper, which
has its own sources, its own developmental logic, and its
own 'laws of motion.'

Finally, when the preparation of this manuscript was
essentially complete, I came across a doctoral dissertation
by the late Joseph Schiebel, dealing with the same materials which are covered in part one of the present volume.[6]
Normally, given my views and my temperament, I would
have polemicized in detail with Schiebel, since I regard his
work as wrong-headed at almost every point, but since the
author was dead and unable to reply, this seemed pointless
and mean-spirited, and I have accordingly not dealt with
his work.

It remains only for me to thank my readers in advance
for their attention, and to request that they communicate
directly with me if they have any strong reactions, or are
aware of relevant data or considerations which I have
omitted without explanation, since I may well be dealing
with the topic again if the intellectual situation warrants it.

Stephen P. Dunn

Part one

DECLINE AND FALL

Introduction

It is characteristic of the Marxist theory of social evolution that it is regarded by its adherents as being at once a *scientific* tool, which, if correctly applied, enables the scholar to predict the course of future events, and a *political* tool enabling the political activist (once again provided that it is correctly applied) to influence this course. This dual nature – cognitive and directive, scientific and political – renders the theory subject to certain internal stresses and shifts of character, as now one aspect and then the other is emphasized. This work will be devoted to the description of a case in which the Marxist theory of social evolution underwent modification from the form in which it had been propounded by Marx, Engels, and certain of their early followers (such as Plekhanov), and was later returned to more or less its original form. This case is that of the so-called Asiatic mode of production – a distinctive form of society, not identifiable with any of the other precapitalist social orders recognized in Marxist doctrine, which in the early 1930s was declared by Soviet scholarly and political authorities never to have existed (although it had been specifically listed by Marx himself as one of the historical forms of society), but which has recently become again the subject of debate among Soviet scholars, some of whom uphold its Marxist legitimacy and/or historical reality. It has been suggested by at least one Western scholar (the late Karl A. Wittfogel), and by some of the participants in the original Soviet debate which led to the abandonment of the concept, that the Asiatic mode of production was removed from the official Soviet–Marxist theoretical arsenal for political reasons. If this is the case, the question arises as to whether it was also restored for political reasons and if it was, what the reasons may be. It is not possible, of course, to provide a firm and unambiguous answer to this question at the present time, but I hope that this work will provide some of the materials for doing so.

The fundamental discovery of the Marxist method of historical analysis is the concept of social orders. For Marxists, the social order is a form of society through which all or a significant part of humanity (with variations and exceptions which in turn must be historically accounted for) has passed, or is now passing, or will pass. Each social order has 'laws of motion' – forms and mechanisms of change and development – peculiar to itself. Generally speaking, each contains both the remnants of previous orders and the undeveloped seeds of future ones. However, socialism cannot develop out of capitalism (as the other social orders do out of their predecessors) because of the resistance of the capitalist state. Each social order, in turn, contains two major classes of phenomena: the 'base,' consisting of all the means and methods – material, intellectual, and organizational – by which people exploit the environment and obtain the means of subsistence from it, and the 'superstructure,' consisting of the political and juridical relationships, philosophical and religious ideas, artistic methods, and the like, prevalent at a particular stage of social development. Broadly speaking, the character of the base determines that of the superstructure, but there is a feedback, the effect of which is particularly marked at advanced stages of social development. The relationships between people which arise in the course of the production of material goods, and which prevail at any particular time and place, are collectively known as a 'mode of production.' For antagonistic social orders – those characterized by the presence of classes whose economic interests are directly opposed to each other and whose interrelations are marked by exploitation (this includes all social orders between the primitive–communal, at one end of the course of historical development, and the communist at the other) – the mode of production includes such factors as the system of rules governing ownership of the means of production, and the means by which the surplus product is taken from the immediate producers for the benefit of the ruling class.[1]

It is clear that, in and of itself, the Marxist method of historical analysis, at least where precapitalist societies are concerned, makes use of concepts formulated at a high level of abstraction, and does not stand or fall by specific factual assertions. However, Marx and Engels, in their works, did make specific statements about the social orders and modes of production which had historically existed, and their statements have in general had normative significance for Soviet scholarship. The classical statement by Marx, from his preface to *Toward a Critique of Political Economy*, reads as follows: 'In broad outlines, Asiatic, ancient, feudal, and modern bourgeois modes of production can be designated as progressive epochs in the economic formation of society.'[2] Marx's listing, it must be noted, includes only the modes of production characteristic of antagonistic social orders; it omits the primitive–communal and communist modes of production. The precapitalist modes of production are described as follows by Mandel:[3]

> 1 *Primitive–communal*: 'a primitive gathering, fishing, and hunting economy in which success is possible only if all co-operate, and in which the results are so meager

that they must be shared approximately equally to avoid death by starvation for some, which would endanger the survival of all by making the entire group too small and weak to function and defend itself.'

2   *Asiatic or Asian*: a 'system . . . in which these communal groups remain, but chieftains, ruling clans, or priest-kings emerge, who perform trading or military or irrigation-directing functions for the whole, and who obtain the material means of life through taxes exacted more or less voluntarily from the communes. At this stage the members of the communes no longer share equally in [their] products, but hold the land more or less jointly, so that the individual on the one hand has the protection of the communal entity and on the other has nothing to gain by seriously improving the parcel he happens to be working for a given season or a group of years.'[4]

3   *'Ancient' or 'Classical' or* (in current Russian usage) *'slaveholding'*: 'in which the world's work is done by slaves, and the slave-owners may philosophize or fight or whatever at leisure.'

4   *Feudal* 'in which the ultimate producer is, in the classical sense, a serf, part of whose time must be given to work for his lord and part . . . remains to him to till his own soil. This division of time applies even if it appears in the somewhat concealed form of quitrent in kind or cash or both.'

Obviously, identification of the mode of production involved in any concrete historical social order may present complex problems, both conceptually and in terms of the interpretation of facts. It is also clear that the identification of a given mode of production has important political implications, since, for example, a political strategy which would be appropriate in the presence of a feudal social order, where the working class might be the temporary ally of the rising bourgeoisie, would be entirely out of place if the feudal social order had already been replaced by a capitalist one. This accounts for the peculiar sharpness and 'stubbornness' (to use a favorite expression of the Russians) of the debates on the identification of social orders and modes of production conducted in the Soviet Union during the 1920s and early 1930s.

Decline and fall: 1929–34

Our account of the discussion between 1929 and approximately 1934, in the course of which[5] the concept of the Asiatic mode of production was authoritatively removed from the Soviet–Marxist theoretical canon, will deal with two main topics, corresponding to the two major temporal phases of the discussion itself. First, we will set forth the substantive arguments raised by the participants in the discussion. Second, we will deal with the handling of those historical phenomena which had previously been subsumed under the Asiatic mode of production, when this concept could no longer be applied to them. In addition, we will have to say something about modifications in the definitions of the other modes of production (feudal and classical, or slave-holding, and in part also primitive–communal) caused by the effort to include in them the phenomena previously handled under the Asiatic mode. Our treatment of this third point, significant and intriguing as it is, cannot be complete within the bounds of this monograph.

The arguments of the participants in the 1929–34 discussion can be conveniently categorized as follows: (1) arguments from authority, subdivisible into (a) positive arguments from positive authority ('Marx himself described the

7

Asiatic mode of production as one of the "progressive epochs in economic formation of society," and we are bound by what he said'), (b) negative arguments from positive authority, either direct ('Lenin specifically rejected the Asiatic mode of production, and we're bound by what he said') or *ex silentio* ('Lenin nowhere endorses the Asiatic mode of production; therefore we're not bound by it regardless of what Marx said'), and (c) negative arguments from negative authority ('Trotsky [or Bukharin or Kautsky or some other recognized deviationist] accepted the Asiatic mode of production; therefore we're bound to reject it'); (2) arguments from pure Marxist theory; and (3) political arguments. These three types are often combined in the pronouncements of a single discussant, and even in a single sentence.

Arguments from authority

Arguments from authority, where Marx and Engels are concerned, are complicated by the peculiarities of their treatment of precapitalist society, which flow from the limitations of the data available to them, and also from the prevailingly polemical origin and form of their works. In the theoretical works published during his lifetime, and under Engels's editorship, during the decade or so following his death, Marx was chiefly concerned with capitalist society, and his intense interest in the earlier stages of history (which caused him to assemble an immense mass of notes and hundreds of pages of completed manuscripts) showed itself mainly in scattered *obiter dicta* on such matters as land tenure, irrigation, and the status of labor. The manuscripts and scattered articles in which he dealt in detail with 'pre-capitalist economic formations' were published or collected in convenient form for the most part after the close of the Soviet discussion in its initial phase. Therefore, the argument from the authority of Marx could not be formulated by the original discussants in as clear-cut a way as by present-day students of the problem.[6]

The handling of the argument from the authority of Marx and Engels in the initial phase of the discussion is marked by a curious paradox. The positive or offensive side of this argument was monopolized by the proponents of the Asiatic mode of production, who were on the defensive politically and eventually 'lost the debate' (at least for the time being). On the other hand, the opponents of the Asiatic mode of production, who had the upper hand politically and presented themselves as super-orthodox Marxists, were compelled to reinterpret or disregard certain clear statements by Marx and Engels – notably the passage from the preface to *Toward a Critique of Political Economy* which has already been quoted. The solutions to this problem offered by the 'anti-Aziatchiki' – the opponents of the Asiatic mode of production – are basically two. The first, and more original and bolder, of these is exemplified by M. Ia. Godes, author of the main paper at the debate organized by the Association of Marxist Orientalists at the Enukidze Oriental Institute in Leningrad, in February of 1931. Faced with a choice (as he sees it) between accepting the Asiatic mode of production and rejecting Marx, Godes opts, with a minimum of hesitation, for the latter course.

> The statement on the Asiatic mode of production cannot be crossed out of Marx's words; our task consists not in blindly repeating this statement, but rather – since our contemporary ideas on the historical development of the countries of the East do not confirm the existence of a specific social order such as the Asiatic mode of production – in explaining how and why Marx at a particular stage in the development of his theory and at a particular stage of development of historical scholarship, expressed views on the social

9

structure of the East, which in some parts of them have not been confirmed.[7]

Godes emphasized the fact that Marx's published statements on the Asiatic mode of production were made before he had encountered L.H. Morgan's writings on ancient society (in fact, before these had been written), and that therefore Marx's theory of the development of society contained very noticeable gaps. Godes interprets Marx's theory of the Asiatic mode of production as a kind of missing link, supplied by Marx in the absence of actual knowledge concerning the development of private property. He also points out – as do most participants in the discussion, in both its earlier and more recent phase – that the later works of Marx and Engels do not mention the Asiatic mode of production.

Those who were not prepared either to reject Marx or to accept the Asiatic mode of production were compelled to find some way of disposing of the inconvenient passages in which Marx appeared to postulate such a mode. The most ingenious and doctrinaire of these orthodox 'anti-Aziatchiki' is S. Iolk. He regards the 'Marxological' aspects of the discussion as secondary, since, once the political unacceptability of the Asiatic mode had been demonstrated, 80 per cent of the necessary work has been done. Iolk begins his discussion of the argument from the authority of Marx, properly so-called, with what he calls a purely literary correction. The current Russian translation of the passage in the introduction of *Toward a Critique of Political Economy* which lists the successive social orders is incorrect; comparison of the German or French versions with the Russian one shows this clearly. The passage should be translated as follows: 'In their general features, the Asiatic, classical, feudal and modern bourgeois modes of production may be considered as progressive epochs in the economic order of society.' The point here is that each

10

of the modes of production mentioned is given in the plural, so that one cannot assume that each of them is one specific thing; rather, each term refers to an entire category. Iolk's conclusion is as follows:

> It follows in my opinion that the term 'mode of production' itself in these formulations is used by Marx not in its broad sense as a definite class structure of combination of relationships of production in society, but in the special sense in which Marx often uses this term. In such expressions for example as 'craft mode of production,' 'communal mode of production,' 'small-scale peasant,' 'manufactory'[8] modes of production. In the introduction what is probably being spoken of is the 'modes of production' in this sense, and I am assuming that, for example, under feudal modes of production Marx understood the 'small-scale peasant' and 'craft,' and under the classical mode of production the 'small-scale peasant' . . . based on slave labor, and under the Asiatic, the 'communal mode of production' and the 'small-scale peasant,' etc.[9]

In other words, Marx in this instance was not writing as a Marxist. This piece of special pleading, whatever its merits in other respects, had the effect of leaving Marx open to the charge of muddled thinking, since the same expression was used in two distinct senses. This point, as we shall see, was not lost on Iolk's opponents.

Iolk does not agree with Godes that Marx developed the idea of a distinctive Eastern socio-economic order in error, having been misled by the bourgeois Orientalists whose works were all that was available to him. Iolk's reason for rejecting this thesis is highly significant. He contends that it is more or less precisely known on what data Marx based himself, and what peculiarities of Oriental society he noted from the sources available to him – namely, ultimate state

11

ownership of the land, wide distribution of a communal system, despotic government, the very important role of artificial irrigation, and a certain backwardness of economic development. But could Marx in fact have asserted the existence of a special social order on the basis of these superficial factors? If, as Godes contends, he did so, then we must conclude that Marx's error was not merely one of fact suggested by current data, but constituted a violation of his own methodology, in that he did not ask himself the question of the relationship between labor and the means of production.

> In order to be logical, Comrade Godes would have in this case to accuse Comrade Mad'iar and his 'school,' not of falsely interpreting Marx's correct views, but on the contrary of correctly repeating Marx's false idea of a special 'Eastern' social order.[10]

While I cannot, in this present analysis, deal in detail with K.A. Wittfogel's critique[11] of Marx's statements on the Asiatic mode of production, it is interesting that Iolk's point here is closely related to Wittfogel's major charge against Marx – namely, that, in violation of his own methodology, he failed to specify the nature of the ruling and exploiting class under this system. It should also be noted that Soviet Marxist theorists in both phases of the discussion fail to be fully consistent in distinguishing between the concept of 'mode of production' (which, properly speaking, includes only the phenomena of the base) and that of 'social order' which takes in both base and superstructure. The point is important, and causes some confusion, since even if one recognizes the Asiatic mode of production as a unitary and identifiable phenomenon, it does not follow that only one kind of social order can arise on the basis of it. On the contrary, political and religious systems as different as those of ancient Mesopotamia, Achaemenid Persia, Mogul India, and imperial China at various stages of its history, have all developed out of the characteristic 'Asiatic' relationships of production as Marx describes them.

If we wish to describe the reception of Iolk's interpretation of Marx's position on the Asiatic mode of production, we are faced with a complex situation. The argument from authority shades off at a number of points into theoretical argument, since, after all, Marx's theory is based on Marx's own insights. On the whole, it cannot be said that Iolk's or Godes's position on the argument from the authority of Marx proved convincing to many participants in this particular discussion – even those who were opposed to the concept of the Asiatic mode of production, or had serious reservations about it from a political point of view.

When we consider the argument from the authority of Lenin, we find a very different state of affairs. Lenin never committed himself personally to the concept of the Asiatic mode of production: all attempts to show that he did so run into the same kind of artificiality as the attempts of the anti-Aziatchiki to dissociate Marx from the concept.

Wittfogel[12] presents Lenin as having accepted the concept of the Asiatic mode of production – albeit with important restrictions and vacillations – from 1894 until 1914, and having reversed his position abruptly at that point. Of the more than thirty points in Lenin's works of the pre-1914 period cited by Wittfogel in support of his interpretation, in so far as it relates specifically to the Asiatic mode of production, all but one (which I will deal with in a moment) fall into one of the following categories: (a) verbatim quotations from the works of Marx and Engels in which Lenin makes no independent comment whatever relative to the Asiatic mode of production; (b) uses of the word 'Asiatic' applied to countries, societies, or individuals in a purely geographical sense; and (c) polemics with others (notably Plekhanov) in which Lenin cites his adversary's use of the term 'Asiatic mode of production,' often placing it in quotation marks, and making clear in the context his own nonacceptance of the concept. It is clear that none of these categories of citations (except perhaps the first)[13] has any probative force relative to the hypothesis that Lenin accepted the concept of the Asiatic mode of production at any stage in his career. It is equally true, as Ter-Akopian points out (see note 4), that he never specifically repudiated it.

The one passage from Lenin which Wittfogel quotes relatively *in extenso*, and which actually says, on its face, what he reports it as saying, occurs in the context of a polemic with Rosa Luxemburg. In this passage, Lenin mentions a number of characteristics which, taken together, yield a concept of 'Asiatic despotism': 'where completely patriarchal, precapitalist features and an insignificant development of a commodity economy and class differentiation prevail in the economy of the given country.'[14] Lenin does not, however, specifically use the term 'Asiatic mode of production,' nor does he make any reference to the absence of private landholding, or the identity between rent and taxes, which would be the fundamental criteria for the existence of this mode of production according to any orthodox Marxist interpretation. The point here is that societies with the characteristics which Lenin lists have in fact existed, but that there is a considerable difference between recognizing this obvious fact and hypostasizing a distinctive mode of production on the basis of it. There is no evidence, either in this passage or anywhere else in Lenin's works, that he ever took the second step.

Wittfogel's discussion of Lenin's attitude toward feudalism presents a different picture: here the references are accurate in themselves, but the interpretation of them goes far beyond Lenin's clear intent. Wittfogel[15] makes much of Lenin's recognition of the differences between Russian feudalism and the Western European variety. Once again, such differences actually exist; they relate primarily to the political structure of the feudal state. For Marxists, however, the decisive factor is not political, but economic – the relation of the immediate producers to the means of production, and the mechanism by which the surplus product is extracted from the immediate producers. One may well recognize that important differences exist between two systems – and one may even hesitate to call them by the same name in ordinary (i.e., non-Marxist) historical terminology – without being prepared to assign them to different modes of production. Furthermore, Lenin's hesitancy about applying the term 'feudalism' to Russian conditions may in some cases have been merely a matter of political prudence. Compare, for example, Wittfogel's rendering of a passage in Lenin with what Lenin actually wrote:

> Noting that the appropriateness of the term 'feudalism' to the Russian middle ages was being questioned, he found it 'least applicable to Russia.'[16]
> 'Feudal-craft . . .' here almost intentionally there is chosen the expression least applicable to Russia, since the applicability of the term feudalism to our middle ages is being questioned.[17]

The original passage at least permits the interpretation that Lenin merely considered it tactically inadvisable to use the term 'feudalism' in this context, inasmuch as there was a dispute about its applicability, but himself took no position on the merits of the question. In fact, the efforts of the Soviet Aziatchiki to enlist the authority of Lenin on their side of the dispute seem rather half-hearted, except in the following case.

In his report on the Stockholm Congress of the RSDRP (Russian Social Democratic Workers' Party), Lenin writes as follows, in the course of a polemic with Plekhanov in regard to the proposed agrarian program of the RSDRP:

15

*First of all, look at this 'nationalization in Muscovy
before the reign of Peter I.' We will not dwell on the fact
that Plekhanov's views on history are an exaggerated
version of the liberal-Narodnik view of Muscovy. It is
absurd to talk about the land being nationalized in
Russia in the period before Peter I; we have only to refer
to Klyuchevsky, Yefimenko and other historians. But let
us leave these excursions into history.* Let us assume for
a moment that the land was really nationalized in
Muscovy before the reign of Peter I, in the 17th
century. What follows from this? According to
Plekhanov's logic, it follows that nationalization would
facilitate the restoration of Muscovy. But such logic is
sophistry and not logic, it is juggling with words without
analyzing the economic basis of development, or the
economic content of concepts. Insofar as (or if) the land
was nationalized in Muscovy the economic basis of this
nationalization was the *Asiatic mode of production*. But
it is the *capitalist mode of production* that became
established in Russia in the second half of the 19th
century and is absolutely predominant in the 20th
century. What, then, remains of Plekhanov's argument?
He confused nationalization based on the Asiatic mode
of production with nationalization based on the
capitalist mode of production. Because the words are
identical he failed to see the fundamental difference in
economic, that is, production relations.[18]

This passage (minus the initial italicized portion) was cited
by a number of the defenders of the Asiatic mode of
production – notably G. Papaian[19] and L. Mad'iar[20] – in
support of the position that Lenin recognized the Asiatic
mode of production. In his closing remarks to the 1931
conference on the Asiatic mode of production, Godes
points out with a good deal of justice that the full quotation
makes it quite clear that Lenin did not believe for a

moment that the land in pre-Petrine Rus' had really been nationalized, and that therefore the question of whether this had occurred under the aegis of the Asiatic mode of production or in some other way was moot. Accordingly, this passage had no probative value with respect to Lenin's position on the Asiatic mode of production.[21]

What has been said in the last few paragraphs does not, of course, prove that Lenin ever explicitly rejected the concept of the Asiatic mode of production. This can be shown only from an argument *ex silentio*, but the argument is stronger than most others of the same type. In his lecture 'The State', delivered in July 1919, his only explicit and connected statement to my knowledge, of his understanding of the Marxist approach to precapitalist society, Lenin makes no allusion whatever to the Asiatic mode of production and presents the sequence of 'antagonistic' social order in the form 'slave-holding–feudal–capitalist,' giving no fourth term.[22] I personally regard this as conclusive on the issue in question.

Since arguments from negative authority are actually political arguments of a rather primitive type, I will confine myself here to pointing out that various participants in the debate on the Asiatic mode of production – not only at the session with which we have been concerned in the last few paragraphs, but also at various other places and in published papers and pamphlets – called attention to the 'pro-Asiatic' position of various recognized deviationists such as Trotsky, Plekhanov, or A.A. Bogdanov, the economist and Marxist theoretician. In most cases the argument from negative authority is not given in direct and unadorned form. Rather, the undesirable political consequences and the intellectual drawbacks of the theory of the Asiatic mode of production are illustrated by reference to the work of Bogdanov or whoever is the polemical target for the moment.

17

Theoretical arguments

In discussing the arguments relative to the Asiatic mode of production which are based on Marxist theory *per se*, we must bear in mind two important considerations. In the first place, the category of theoretical argument cannot be separated with absolute clarity from that of arguments from authority, since the theoretical debate takes place within terms of reference formally agreed to by all parties, and these terms of reference have been established by Marx (and to a lesser degree by Engels). Second, the theoretical argument relative to the Asiatic mode of production almost never appears in pure form, since the theoretical argument against this concept usually takes the form of an attempt to account by other means for the phenomena which the 'Aziatchiki' attribute to the Asiatic mode of production.

On the whole it can be said that, as with the arguments from authority, the initiative in the theoretical arguments belongs in important respects to the proponents of the Asiatic mode of production. Its opponents are forced to do violence in different ways and to varying degrees to the basic principles of the Marxist theory of history. Furthermore, the most serious objections to the concept of the Asiatic mode of production do not appear to have been recognized, or fully analyzed, during the early stage of the debate, even by its opponents. For convenience of exposition, let us discuss first the positive arguments, those in favor of the Asiatic mode of production. We will then consider the negative arguments – those against the concept of the Asiatic mode of production – followed by the rebuttals to the latter. As we will see, the rebuttal arguments show certain obvious or subtle changes in emphasis and tactics relative to the original positive arguments.

Perhaps the most forthright and systematic defender of the Asiatic mode of production is S.I. Kovalev – a prominent historian of classical antiquity who afterwards wrote the standard Soviet text (still used) on the history of the ancient world, and became head of the Museum of Religion and Atheism in Leningrad. It is interesting that, like some other participants in the discussion on the paper by Godes to which I have already referred, Kovalev describes himself as a recent convert to the theory of the Asiatic mode of production; his conversion was the result of recent intensive study of the works of Marx and Engels. From this study he concluded that the existence of dispersed, or noncollective, landownership is central to the concept of feudalism developed by Marx and that where the ownership of land has a different character (as it did in India, ancient China, and the states of the ancient Near East), feudalism in the proper sense cannot be said to have existed. If we disregard this point, what we obtain is a definition of feudalism almost identical to that advanced by Max Weber, which involves the existence of a class of privileged landowners exploiting another class of dependent immediate producers, but omits any mention of the form and character of the ownership of land.

The opponents of the Asiatic mode of production rely chiefly on two classical quotations from Marx's *Capital* which run as follows:

> The specific economic form, in which unpaid surplus labor is pumped out of direct producers, determines the relationship of rulers and ruled, as it grows directly out of production itself and, in turn, reacts upon it as a determining element. . . . It is always the direct relationship of the owners of the conditions of production to the direct producers . . . which reveals the innermost secrets, the hidden basis of the entire social structure.[23]

> That special character and means by which this union [of the producer with the means of production] is effected distinguishes the various economic epochs of social structure from each other.

Kovalev's comment on his quotations is as follows:

These quotations, comrades, are well known to all of us. They are by Marx. And if Marx nevertheless recognized the Asiatic mode of production there are only two ways out: either Marx was *methodologically* mistaken (which I don't admit, and you will hardly admit either) or else the matter is not as simple as you seem to think. Obviously the matter at issue *is not only* the method of uniting the producer with the means of production. Otherwise Marx could not have established a difference in principle between the feudal and the 'Asiatic' forms of exploitation, since in both cases we have a relatively similar means of uniting the producers with the means of production (the producer is allotted land on a de facto basis) – and Marx saw this as well as we do. Consequently, the means of uniting or the form of exploitation cannot be understood in a too general sense, but must be made as concrete as possible. If the form of exploitation is understood 'sociologically' – or, in other words, à la Weber – then any kind of exploitation of the 'dependent unarmed population' by a privileged group of landowners through the appropriation of precapitalist rent will be feudal exploitation, and in that case the Asiatic mode of production, the feudal, and even the classical [i.e., Greco-Roman] can be thrown into one pile. If the form of exploitation is understood according to Marx, historically – i.e., concretely – then we must take account, comrades, of how the property is divided in this case, and of how rent is appropriated, and of what is the basis of its appropriation, and of how it is distributed; and in that case, we obtain not two but three precapitalist social orders.[24]

The reader should bear in mind, first, that the social order which Kovalev, and most other participants in this discussion, refer to as 'classical' (*antichnyi*) is usually called 'slaveholding' by Soviet scholars today; and, second, that the three social orders to which Kovalev refers at the end of this quotation are 'Asiatic,' classical or slaveholding, and feudal. Primitive–communal society is generally not thought by Soviet scholars to represent a social order in the same sense as the others, because it does not involve exploitation. I have dealt with this point in some detail elsewhere, and will not touch upon it here.[25] It would appear that the renaming of the 'classical' social order as 'slaveholding' was at least partly due to the series of developments being described here, as a result of which the societies of the ancient East (China, India, Mesopotamia, and Egypt, among others) were assigned to the same broad category as those of the Mediterranean Basin.

Kovalev proceeds to defend the concept of the Asiatic mode of production in a quite straightforward way as a necessary component of the Marxist theory of history. He contends that if the Asiatic mode of production is abandoned the result will be a fundamental revision of the Marxian interpretation of the historical process as it has existed up to that point. Stripped of collateral issues and polemical asides, the argument runs this way: the historical process is characterized by a progression of the same kind in all parts of the world. This unilinearity must not be understood in a vulgar way, nor does it exhaust the historical process. Both Marx and Engels recognized parallel and collateral processes, but the main trunk of development was the same. However, historical development not only is unilinear but also proceeds in a straight line, which again must not be understood in an oversimplified way.

If we subsume the Asiatic mode of production under the concept of feudalism, what we obtain is not a Marxist model, but the model which is very popular among bourgeois scholars; . . . in place of a unified process, we obtain a multiplicity of historical processes – i.e., a mechanistic conception. If we consider the Asiatic mode of production feudal, then we must consider early classical [Greco-Roman] society feudal as well, since it also is based, according to Marx, on collective exploitation and collective possession [of the means of production]. Thus, feudalism will turn out for us to be listed both before the classical mode of production and after it, and we will fall from the straight path into the embrace of the reactionary theory of cycles.[26]

This is the capstone of the argument in favor of the Asiatic mode of production. In conclusion, Kovalev (and in this he is typical of the better-informed and more sophisticated Aziatchiki) rejects all contentions to the effect that the state in the ancient East was of a supra-class nature. The exploiting class in societies marked by the Asiatic mode of production consisted of a privileged group of officials, warriors, and landowning priests – or, more precisely, people living on land rent. These people were directly organized into the state, owned the means of production collectively, and collectively exploited the members of the primitive rural communes. Kovalev admits that this is similar to feudalism in the proper sense (under which the ruling class also lived on land rent); on the other hand, it is also similar to the classical mode of production – particularly during the early period when so-called classical state ownership of land existed – and in general to all precapitalist modes of production. In order to be consistent, the opponents of the Asiatic mode of production must liquidate the differences between all precapitalist social orders and unite them into a single formation. It is significant that, as we will see further on, some recent writers have also advocated this procedure.

Kovalev's arguments carried the day in one important

respect. While the Asiatic mode of production was rejected, apparently largely for political reasons, the point of view which defined the ancient Eastern societies as feudal was not openly defended after about 1933–4, except by one or two individual scholars. Rather, these societies were considered as belonging to the 'slaveholding' social order – a solution which brought with it other difficulties, almost equally severe. It is worthy of special note that Kovalev's contention to the effect that the rejection of the Asiatic mode of production leads to a circular conception of the historical process went unanswered in this particular debate, and also, as far as I can tell, in the other debates of this period.

The theoretical opposition to the Asiatic mode of production took a number of different forms at various times. The most prominent of these was the attempt to redefine feudalism by abstracting from the specific political forms taken by this system under European conditions – the hierarchy of suzerain and vassals at various levels, the connection between the ownership of land and political authority over the people living on it, the delegation of various aspects of state authority to feudal lords of various kinds, and the like. In itself, this redefinition of feudalism makes good sense in Marxist terms, since all of the features that I have mentioned belong to the superstructure, and not to the base, which in principle determines the nature of the social order. However, this tactic creates other difficulties in addition to the problem of a circular historical process which was just mentioned. For example, S.M. Dubrovskii, one of the most convinced and persistent opponents of the concept of the Asiatic mode of production – he was still maintaining, in 1966, shortly before his death, the same flatly negative position which he occupied during the debate of 1929–31 – feels obliged, in combating this concept, to posit an additional social order, marked by serfdom, of which Marx makes no mention. In fact, Dubrovskii lists in all no fewer than ten separate social orders of which his discussion is concerned only with the first six.[27] Of these six social orders, two fall within the sphere of primitive–communal society, which was not included by Marx in his list. However, even allowing for this change, a glance at Dubrovskii's list will suffice to show the sharp difference from the one given by Marx. Historically, the first social order cited by Dubrovskii is that of primitive society, based on the clan. The second is patriarchal society where each peasant household is relatively autonomous, and relationships of production going beyond the bounds of the household are almost or totally absent. The third social order is that of slaveholding society, which, according to Marx, 'passes through a metamorphosis from the patriarchal system mainly for home use to the plantation system for the world market.'[28] The fourth stage is the feudal economy, where the subsistence farming of the immediate producer is dominant, in conjunction with home industry, and these two taken together produce both the necessary and the surplus product. Under this system, exploitation takes place by the charging of rent to the immediate producer, chiefly in kind, partly in money, and only occasionally in labor. The fifth stage is the serf economy, based on *corvée* labor, under which the serf's farm is only an appendage of the landlord's operation. Under this system, the serf produced the necessary product on his own farm, and the surplus product on the landlord's estate, using means of production which (except, of course, for the land) belonged to the serf. The sixth form is represented by the peasant or 'petty-producer' economy, which was characteristic on the one hand of certain periods of classical antiquity, and, on the other, of certain modern population groups, such as the English yeomanry and the Swedish, French, and western German peasantry. It is clear that this model gives rise to severe difficulties, due in part to the very vague definition of the slaveholding order, and, in part, to the extremely broad concept of the petty-producer economy, which is, furthermore, historically discontinuous. It seems to me that Dubrovskii tried to eliminate the Asiatic mode of production by rechristening it as feudalism, and to legitimize this procedure by rechristening what had previously been called feudalism as the 'serf' social order. Dubrovskii maintains that it is the relationships of dominance and subjection, which, by their presence or absence, are diagnostic for the social order. If these relationships are entirely lacking, and if the individual peasant families are not connected or exploited by any superordinate power, then we are in the presence of the patriarchal clan society without classes.

If on the other hand there are relationships of dominance and subjection, then we have either feudalism or serfdom. We are not speaking in the given case about a slave economy. *The slave system presupposes slaves, and not immediate producers*, autonomous or dependent serfs who, however, even in the presence of serfdom, carry on along with the corvée economy of the landowner their own petty immediate subsistence production.[29]

Before proceeding to consider the rebuttal to Dubrovskii's position (and in general the theoretical rebuttal by the supporters of the Asiatic mode of production), we should note two general points. The first of these is the extremely limited nature of Dubrovskii's discussion, and in some respects this applies to that of other participants in the debate as well. The debate appears to be carried on largely in a vacuum as far as data are concerned. In fact, Dubrovskii explicitly recognizes as much.[30] With the exception of the Sinologists such as Mad'iar, Kokin, and Papaian, whose work has not so far been accessible to me, the participants seem to be limiting themselves consciously to the data-base which was available to Marx and Engels. In the case of

Dubrovskii, even his citations to Marx are curiously one-sided: they are limited for the most part to *Capital* and one or two passages from *Toward a Critique of Political Economy*. The second point is that neither Dubrovskii nor most of the other participants in the debate make any attempt at a detailed analysis of the political economy of slavery, although within a period of three or four years after these debates, the 'slaveholding interpretation' of ancient Eastern society became almost universal in Soviet scholarship and remained so until the middle 1960s.

Dubrovskii's position did not go unchallenged. At a special discussion on Dubrovskii's pamphlet held apparently some time during 1929 (the exact date is not indicated),[31] the main speaker, Malyshev, points out forcefully that Dubrovskii's distinction between feudalism and serfdom has no basis in Marx. Nor do the other speakers – even those who do not operate from a specifically Aziatchik position – accept Dubrovskii's contentions. The major and most cogent objection is that Dubrovskii is driven by his static concept of the social order and its components, to keep multiplying social orders and *uklads*.[32] Curiously enough, Dubrovskii runs into heavy fire on this issue from a speaker with the appropriate name of N. Zor'kii ('vigilant'), who presents himself as a super-orthodox Marxist. In commenting on the paper by Efimov (but aiming beyond him at Dubrovskii, who in some respects takes a similar position), Zor'kii points out that the latter's handling of the difference between *uklad* and social order 'is fraught with the crudest kind of political mistakes.'[33] The original passage by Efimov is worth quoting for the light it sheds on the 'ground-rules' of this type of argument; I have indicated in brackets the annotations and additions to the stenographic record made by the author before publication.

Thus, we define a social order by that type of relations which leaves its impress on the survivals of all previous relations and the rudiments of future ones. Any social order is a variegated phenomenon, but one which has one general envelope which is determined by the prevailing state of production. [For the final publication, the author replaced the words 'social order' with the word 'society,' and the words 'variegated phenomenon having one general envelope' with the words 'a variegated whole.'] Among the *uklads* in the Marxist literature it is customary to list not only the survivals of a particular social order as such, but even a particular fragment of social orders which have certain differences (though not decisive ones) in their structure. Thus, for example, state capitalism is not an independent social order, but it characterizes a peculiar stage in the development and decay of capitalism. For example, under socialism there are retained elements of state capitalism, and they enter into the makeup of the first phase of communist society. This means that here the *uklad* is applied to a more specific phenomenon. [The author added to the final text at this point a comment to the effect that this formulation repeated the same mistake made above (see the earlier bracketed passage inserted in this quotation) and was furthermore unfortunate with regard to state capitalism, because the state capitalism which obtained in Germany during the First World War was simply ordinary capitalism in a special stage and under special wartime conditions, while 'in the USSR, state capitalism is an *uklad* which in 1921 was an ally of the socialist *uklad*, and is now in the stage of being broken by the socialist *uklad*.'] But we must separate from the socio-economic order those features such as usurious and commercial capital, which are neither social orders nor *uklads* of society.[34]

As examples to illustrate the structure of social orders, Efimov points to the existence, in the mountains of Svanetia in the Transcaucasus, of 'socialist competition

27

between clans,' and to the Witoto Indian tribe of South America, whose chief acts as an agent of the rubber company. In the first case the clan *uklad* of the Svan mountaineers is deformed under the influence of the socialist *uklad*, although one cannot yet speak of a socialist social order or the first stage of the communist one. The primitive–communal order of the Witotos enters as an *uklad* into the world capitalist system, and undergoes deformation by it. All this does not sit well with Zor'kii, who appears to fear (perhaps with some justice) that by this method of argument, the unitary, orthodox–Marxist concept of the social order will be broken down into a number of interchangeable components, and will no longer be seen as a separate historical phenomenon, possessing its own 'laws of motion.' What is particularly interesting is that Zor'kii seems to see the dangers of this position in specifically political terms, rather than in theoretical ones. 'If Comrade Efimov imagines that the socialist social order already exists, then Dubrovskii made a similar mistake by listing in his catalogue of social orders the economy of the transitional period [of Soviet society] as a special mode of production.'[35] Thus, we find the Asiatic mode of production being defended (even if indirectly) on basically political grounds, little more than a year before a full-scale political attack was mounted against it.

The central theoretical point at issue, however, is a more subtle one, and also more significant: there appears to be a constant temptation to think of the social orders not as descriptions of actual historical states of affairs, but as logical categories or 'ideal types,' somewhat in the manner of Max Weber. Such logical categories, having no real objective existence, can combine and recombine in ways which are not subject to the type of descriptive historical law which Marx and his more orthodox followers have postulated. This error is called 'Bogdanovism' by its Soviet critics during this period, after A.A. Bogdanov (real name,

Malinovskii), a prominent although somewhat heterodox Marxist theorist of the earlier Soviet period, and a co-author of one of the first standard textbooks of Marxist political economy.[36] Another viewpoint described as Bog-danovist by critics of the concept of the Asiatic mode of production (although there is scant justification for this in Bogdanov's own work, as far as I can discover) is that which attributes to the despotic Eastern state a 'supra-class' character, and derives the power of the bureaucracy from its socially useful function in regulating the construc-tion and use of the irrigation network. In fact, Dubrovskii, in his rebuttal during the 1929 debate, says rather plain-tively that he did not set out, in his pamphlet, to discover America, but only wished to refute those who consider Eastern despotism to be of a supra-class nature.[37] Suppor-ters of the concept of the Asiatic mode of production reject with some heat the imputation that they underestimate the extent of class antagonism within this system. For example, Kovalev maintains that societies based on the Asiatic mode of production were quite clearly class societies, the exploit-ing class being made up of a privileged group of officials, warriors, and landowning priests – or in more general terms, people living on land rent.[38] In a superficial sense, this statement is quite justified. However, two comments are called for. First, the uneasiness of many Marxist scho-lars about the class nature of Eastern despotism is based on a valid question – though one which does not emerge as clearly as it might in the debate. When we read Wittfogel's description of Oriental despotism, or the passage quoted in note 36, we are driven to wonder (if we wish to continue thinking in Marxist categories) what was the source of the despot's power, and whose interests were represented by the state which he headed. Assertions about the corporate structure of the ruling class in ancient Oriental society do not ultimately answer this question, since even if we grant the point, we must then ask how one gained access to the

ruling corporation. Second, although classical Marxist doctrine holds that the state, in fully developed class society, is
always, everywhere, and inevitably an organ of class domination, Engels nevertheless did raise the possibility that
certain functions of the state might in some instances ante-
date the origin of class society.[39]. Although the passage in
question is not cited during the phase of the debate with
which we are presently dealing, it does tend to explain
certain assertions, which otherwise appear paradoxical, to
the effect that the social order governed by the Asiatic
mode of production was the final phase of the primitive–communal order, or at least that Marx regarded
it as such.[40]

Political arguments

My discussion of the political arguments on the Asiatic
mode of production will be schematic and will not attempt
to dig beneath the surface of the published debates, which
at this point in history, would be largely a speculative
enterprise. There are two important comments to be made
before we embark on the substance of the matter. First, the
published debate leaves the definite impression that the
validity of the Asiatic mode of production as a tool of
Marxist analysis was an open question in a political sense at
the time. None of the speakers gives any sign of being
under political (as opposed to doctrinal) constraint. By this
I mean that all participants in the debate were, or felt,
obliged to couch their arguments in acceptable Marxist
terms, and to support them with appropriate authorities,
but that all felt at liberty to determine for themselves,
within broad limits, what terms were acceptable and what
authorities were appropriate. This does not mean that
political arguments were not used, or that, when used, they
were not in some cases resented, but they do not seem to
have had any particular intimidating effect. Second, the

political arguments on the question of the Asiatic mode of production must be divided into two categories, which we may call, for want of more precise terms, the general and the specific. General political arguments on this point maintain that either the maintenance or the denial of the Asiatic mode of production as the basis of a particular social order compromise the general validity and intellectual integrity of the Marxist method, and hence make it a less effective political tool. There is little doubt in my mind that Dubrovskii's anti-Aziatchik position, summarized in the preceding section, is based on a general political argument, and it is significant that Zor'kii's rebuttal of this position operates basically within the same terms. *Specific* political arguments, on the other hand, maintain that a particular theoretical position has political implications which are undesirable in terms of the situation at a given point in time. The positions taken by Godes, Iolk, and some other speakers during the 1930 debate are based on specific political arguments, most of which relate to the question of the appropriate strategy for the Chinese revolution.

Godes begins his introductory paper to the 1930 debate by making a political analysis of the question of the Asiatic mode of production in relation to Chinese events. He recalls that during the debate on the report of the Soviet delegation to the Comintern, Lominadze, in a speech on the Chinese revolution, maintained that the type of relations existing in the Chinese countryside could be called feudalism only in a very conditional way, with the qualification that it does not resemble the conditions of the European Middle Ages. Lominadze wished to call these relationships the Asiatic mode of production, as Marx had, but Godes protests that although this may seem like a harmless terminological correction, Lominadze had in fact, in describing the character of the Canton commune, given a Trotskyist interpretation, defining the tasks of the revolution as those of a socialist one. The precise words used by Godes at this point deserve close attention: 'It turns out that the denial of feudalism in China, or the theory of it, always leads to political errors, and errors of an essentially Trotskyist order.'[41]

The essential point, therefore, is not the *presence* of the Asiatic mode of production, but the *absence* of feudalism. One is tempted to wonder whether the speakers who took this political tack were concerned to maintain the validity of the Soviet-sponsored alliance between the Chinese Communist Party and the Kuomintang, which would have been defensible under feudal conditions, but not under capitalist ones, such as Radek and some of his followers believed existed in China at the time. The same concern emerges even more clearly in the opening pages of Iolk's address,[42] where he attacks a recent book by E.S. Varga, *Ocherki po ekonomike Kitaia*, which has so far remained inaccessible to me. Varga apparently maintained that land rent in China had a usurious capitalist character rather than a feudal one. In accordance with this view, he denied the existence in China of a class of feudal landowners – which was the same thing that Trotsky said in *The Permanent Revolution*. Varga's conclusion from this is that there was in China no opposition between the bourgeoisie and the feudal landowners such as existed in Europe, and that therefore (in accordance with the views of Trotsky and Radek) the working class and the peasantry would be allied in China not against two classes but against one – namely the bourgeoisie.

Kokin, one of the chief defenders of the Aziatchik position, mounts a vigorous counter-attack on the issue of Trotskyist influence, proving, at least to his own satisfaction, that it is beside the point.

[The] very widespread attempts to connect the Asiatic mode of production with Trotskyism are no more than

a widely used demagogic method. First of all,
Trotskyism denies the presence of feudalism in China *at
present*, which we do not do, and which absolutely does
not follow from the Asiatic mode of production. In the
second place, Trotskyism – and I consider it necessary
to emphasize this – denies feudal relations in China at
present by no means because of the recognition of the
Asiatic mode of production. If we take the most
colorful representative of the Trotskyist Opposition –
so to speak, the chieftain of Trotskyism on the Chinese
question (I'm speaking of Comrade Radek) – we will
see that Radek, in the first place, denied and still denies
the existence of the Asiatic mode of production in the
historical past in China, holding that in China feudalism
existed beginning with the most ancient historical
times; in the second place Radek, in denying the
existence of feudalism at present, holds that in
contemporary China, commercial capital prevailed. . . .
I hold that the struggle for the purity of
Marxist-Leninist theory in Oriental studies has to be
conducted on two fronts. First of all, against those who
try to fit the history of the development of the Eastern
colonial and semi-colonial countries in under the course
of development passed through by the European
countries in their history; and secondly, against those
who speak of an absolute peculiarity, of an
'exceptionality' of the countries of the East and against
those who thereby nourish the evaluation of the East as
a region of 'exoticism' – as an area into which
civilization must be 'imported'.[43]

It should be carefully noted (though it is hardly cause for
astonishment) that Kokin here is not defending the Trotskyist position *per se*, but is differentiating the Aziatchik
position from it. On the other hand, his reasoning is
straightforward, and his tone is by no means apologetic.

As might be expected, Iolk impatiently rejects these arguments as sophisms. His reaction is worth quoting as an example of what might be called the 'early Bolshevik' attitude toward history as a discipline.

> I have cited these facts[44] not in order to discredit politically the adherents of the special 'Asiatic' mode of production, but in order that every comrade who is coming into contact for the first time with the essence of this theory should show a definite caution, and that every revolutionary, Marxist, and Bolshevik who attempts to approach the analysis of this theory from the point of view of its methodological value should have a particular party prejudice in regard to it.[45]

It would not be fair to call this position a Stalinist one (as some would no doubt be inclined to do), since Lenin said very similar things on many occasions, and since in any case what Iolk says here follows directly from the 'unity of theory and practice,' and from the dual nature of Marxism as both a cognitive tool and a political weapon, which was referred to at the beginning of this book. In the next section, we will have occasion to note a definite change in the character of the Marxist methodology, as understood by at least some Soviet scholars, from the sharply focused political weapon which it represented in the hands of Iolk and some of his contemporaries to a more general set of assumptions which *in itself* is compatible with a number of different results. It is, however, striking that despite the polemical sharpness of Iolk and some other speakers, the political arguments even in the 1930 debates do not proceed all in one direction. In his opening paper, Godes comments rather wryly on the efforts of some of his opponents to make the Asiatic mode of production an article of Marxist faith.

Even before the discussion, Comrade Papaian tried to

convince me that inasmuch as the Comintern program talks about the Asiatic mode of production, therefore I am obliged to recognize it exactly as I am obliged to pay my party dues in an exemplary way. We are going to talk about the Comintern program in a little while.[46] Here I would like only to note that I am not one of those who are prepared to consider my opponents Trotskyists merely because they recognize the Asiatic mode of production, but for me any theory is important not for what the author's opinion of it is, but for where it leads and for what conclusions necessarily flow from its application to the contemporary East.[47]

Before proceeding to deal with the next phase of the debate, I want to draw the reader's attention to a very curious aspect of the situation at this point, and also to pose a question to which the sources I have seen provide no obvious or clear-cut answer. As we have seen, the debate at this point is not hampered by any absolute political constraints, although some of the notes struck in it have a threatening sound in the light of later events. I have not been able to find in the published record any specific reference to an authoritative decision on any level to the effect that the concept of the Asiatic mode of production is no longer to be considered a legitimate tool of Marxist inquiry. The most that recent Soviet and East European writers will say, in reviewing the history of Soviet Oriental studies and historical research generally, is that from the early 1930s onward, free discussion was inhibited by political factors.[48] Wittfogel cites Stalin's *Short Course* as having authoritatively ended all discussion on the Asiatic mode of production, which is true enough; but this was not published until eight years after the time with which we are dealing, and Wittfogel specifically declares the process by which the 'ideological blackout' on the Asiatic mode of production was established to be outside the scope of his work.[49] It is of course quite possible that word was simply passed through the academic grapevine that the topic of the Asiatic mode of production was now taboo and that certain positions were no longer safe to take, and that everyone immediately fell into line without incident or comment. However, in view of the liveliness with which the Asiatic mode of production had been discussed previous to this, one would expect to find an explicit recantation by some scholar somewhere.

It is now time to raise a complex and puzzling question which, as it were, sums up within itself the entire development, both intellectual and political, with which we have been dealing in the first part of this book. If, as the material just set forth seems to indicate, those who took the anti-Aziatchik position in the debates of the late 1920s and early 1930s saw the major political danger, not in advocacy of the concept of the Asiatic mode of production *per se*, but in the denial of the feudal character of the ancient Eastern (and particularly the Chinese) social order, then what conclusions are we to draw from the fact that the feudal interpretation of ancient Eastern society generally (but not of that of China)[50] was abandoned almost immediately afterwards and replaced by a 'slaveholding' one – apparently for reasons internal to the Marxist theory of history as an intellectual system? One would think that, if the feudal interpretation of ancient Eastern society as a whole had been considered politically necessary, it would have been insisted on regardless of intellectual consequences, particularly under the conditions of rigid ideological control which supposedly existed during the period of Stalin's undisputed ascendancy. If, on the other hand, it was the interpretation of *Chinese* society specifically which was politically crucial, it would seem sufficient to declare the concept of the Asiatic mode of production inapplicable to the Chinese case, leaving the rest of the model undisturbed, and thus avoiding the difficulties to which the slaveholding interpretation afterwards gave rise. It must be borne in mind that the feudal interpretation, as applied to ancient China and India, does not involve the difficulties encountered in certain other areas (Egypt, Achaemenid and Sassanid Persia, Mesopotamia, and in general the territories occupied by the successor states of Alexander the Great's empire), where this interpretation produces a 'cyclical' version of the historical process, with an obvious – or at least generally recognized – slaveholding society following upon a feudal one.

In the first part of this work, I have attempted to give a historical account, as straightforward as possible, of the process by which the concept of the Asiatic mode of production was rejected as a tool of Marxist analysis, and some of the reasons for this rejection as they were perceived at the time. It would be a considerable mistake, in my opinion, to regard the concept of the Asiatic mode of production as either an unequivocally necessary part of the Marxist theory of history or something unmistakably called for by the historical evidence; accordingly, it would be mistaken to regard the rejection of this concept as an unmitigated intellectual tragedy or as evidence of the complete stultification of the Marxist method (as Wittfogel appears to do). The events following upon the rejection of the Asiatic mode of production, and particularly upon the revival of the discussion in 1964, will, I believe, clearly show that such simplistic judgments are not adequate; these events will be reviewed in part two.

Part two

RESURGENCE

In part one, I traced the process by which the concept of the Asiatic mode of production was removed from the theoretical toolkit used by Soviet Marxist scholars. I closed with some speculations as to the reasons which might have led to this removal; the final section also pointed out certain difficulties which stand in the way of a straightforward political interpretation of the process. In Part two, I will be concerned with the subsequent evolution of the Soviet-Marxist theory of history as it relates to the precapitalist social orders, and particularly with the partial revival of the concept of the Asiatic mode of production beginning in the middle 1960s.

The process leading to this partial revival possesses intellectual characteristics rather different from those of the debates during the early 1930s on the same topic. Instances of overt political argument (with a few questionable exceptions which will be noted below) are not found. Arguments from authority, while they do occur, are considerably more subtle than before, and take different forms. More important than these points, however, is the fact that the entire method and basis of argument has changed. As was pointed out earlier, the discussions of the late 1920s and early 1930s were conducted largely in terms of exegesis of the statements of Marx, Engels, and Lenin; the citation of concrete data was limited to what was necessary in order to characterize a society or a situa-

41

tion, so that it could be seen what Marxist categories applied to it and in what form they should be applied.[1] Some exegetical work is still done,[2] and the Marxist classics are still extensively quoted, but the main emphasis now is on the extraction and interpretation of concrete data in a number of fields with long and complex traditions of research (ancient Egypt, ancient and medieval India, Mesopotamia, Achaemenid and Sassanid Persia, and, in a somewhat different sense, the Western Roman Empire). While these data are still interpreted in terms of a single 'master hypothesis,' there is a good deal of individual variation in the interpretation of the hypothesis, and indeed, some sharp revisions have recently been suggested in the hypothesis itself.[3] The arguments are becoming more and more complex and technical, and, with a few notable exceptions, they show at least the appearance of scholarly objectivity. In one sense, this represents merely the normal process of advance in any field of knowledge, and we would be greatly disappointed if we did not find it, but in another sense it betokens a fundamental change in the character of the Marxist ideology as applied in the Soviet Union, to say nothing of its use in other countries.

Interregnum: 1934–64

As noted at the end of part one, during the year 1933 the discussion on the Asiatic mode of production as such came to an abrupt halt, which in some senses has not yet been satisfactorily explained. After that point, references to the Asiatic mode of production are relatively infrequent, and are stereotyped in a negative sense when they do occur. When the first phase of the debate ended, those who took the 'anti-Aziatchik' position were still maintaining that the ancient Eastern social order had to be considered essentially feudal. When the next phase opened, with the presentation and discussion of a paper by V.V. Struve on the origin and development of the slaveholding system in the ancient East,[4] the proponents of the feudal interpretation of ancient Eastern society were already definitely on the defensive, and the groundwork had been laid for a treatment of the ancient Eastern social order as falling essentially into the slaveholding category. Since this sharp change in the direction of the discussion was largely Struve's work, it will be worth while to consider briefly his intellectual evolution, and the factors which (by his own account) brought him to the position which he occupied at this point. This account will also include a brief summary of his participation in the earlier discussions, with which we have already dealt.

Vasilii Vasil'evich Struve (1889–1965) was a member of the last contingent of Russian scholars to receive the bulk of their professional training under pre-Revolutionary conditions. Originally trained as an Egyptologist, he studied under B.A. Turaev in Moscow and under Adolf Ermann in Berlin. During the late 1920s and early 1930s, he took an increasingly active part in Soviet research on the civilizations of the ancient East, at the same time training himself in Marxism and expanding his scholarly interest from Egypt to the countries of the Fertile Crescent. By the mid-1930s he was one of a relatively small group of Soviet scholars who actually possessed the linguistic and other technical resources for independent research in this complex field.[5] In view of Struve's professional prominence at the time in question, and also in view of later developments, it is significant that during the 1930 discussion on the Godes paper he took an Aziatchik, or at least anti-feudal, position, though one which is carefully qualified. Struve describes himself as a fairly recent convert to the theory of the Asiatic mode of production: when he first heard Godes's paper, some three years previously, he agreed completely with Godes, but after that he began to have doubts, and came to a rather different conclusion – namely that in Egypt there existed a peculiar social order, which could not be called feudal. On the methodological plane, Struve calls attention to the famous passage in the third volume of *Capital* where Marx defines the precapitalist economic forms of the extraction of the unpaid surplus product from the immediate producer. Where there is feudal landed property and rent in labor, the immediate producer works with his own means of production, and carries on his farming independently. Where, as in the ancient Asian societies, there is no private landownership, and the state takes the rent directly, rent and taxes coincide. These two social orders – namely the one where private feudal property exists, and the other where it does not – are contrasted to the slaveholding social order, where presumably the slave has no means of production, and in fact does not even own his own person.

> I am assuming that any assertion to the effect that Marx, in speaking of the Asiatic mode of production, was not referring to a social order, is in fact mistaken. . . . And it is characteristic that it was precisely Comrade Godes, three years ago, who pointed out in his paper that Marx in fact spoke of a socio-economic order. It follows from this that Marx did not distinguish sharply between the Asiatic and feudal modes of production. If we say that everything is feudalism, then we get a feudal porridge in the literal sense from Babylon up to Napoleon . . . . I hold that the accusation against those persons who are proponents of the theory of the Asiatic mode of production – insofar as they emphasize its class character – to the effect that they are opponents of the Marxist method, is certainly

incorrect, agreeing in this respect with what Comrade Kovalev has said.[6]

It is worth noting that the portion of this passage which precedes the second ellipsis reiterates (although less specifically) the position taken by Kovalev in the same debate. Struve attributes the marked organizational differences between the social order of the ancient Eastern countries (particularly Egypt) and that of medieval Europe to specific natural factors which made necessary the construction of large-scale public works, and forced the ruling class to resort to a specialized and very powerful bureaucratic organization, in order to extract as much surplus product as possible from the immediate producers. On this basis it would seem that Struve regarded the social order based on the Asiatic mode of production as a mere local variant of the feudal one, and that therefore his rejection (both at that time and later) of the feudal interpretation showed a fundamental inconsistency in his position.

In the paper on slaveholding relationships in ancient Mesopotamia, presented at the State Academy for the History of Material Culture in 1933 and published in its transactions in 1934, both Struve's position and his methodology have undergone fundamental changes. He now holds that the bulk of the productive labor both in Egypt and in Mesopotamia was done by persons who worked the year around on the royal estates and had no means of production of their own, and who could therefore not be serfs. This view is validated on the basis of analysis of the accounting documents from the Third Dynasty of Ur, as assembled and interpreted by the French scholar Genouillac, and (as far as the Egyptian data are concerned) by a reinterpretation of the standard hieroglyphic sources. With respect to Egypt, Struve concludes that while the slaves were less numerous than free laborers on the communal fields, their labor predominated in the economy, since they worked the year around, while the free laborers worked only four months at a time. According to the standard Soviet–Marxist typology of labor, which is still used,[7] the Mesopotamian year-round laborers, lacking means of production of their own, must be either slaves or hired hands. However, in the accounting documents, hired laborers in the strict sense (a very small number) are listed separately. Further, in another monograph (which I have not seen) Struve is said to show that a word in ancient Egyptian which was previously interpreted to mean 'salary' or pay for labor actually refers to the work itself and not to the compensation, and therefore cannot be used as evidence for the existence of hired labor on any large scale previous to the Macedonian conquest.[8] In some later works, which will be dealt with below, Struve rejected, on philological grounds, the interpretation of certain ancient Egyptian tests (the so-called 'grants of immunity') as showing the presence of essentially feudal relationships.

I am of course in no position to pass on the technical merits of Struve's arguments – nor is it, in the present instance, necessary to do so. The importance of Struve's work during the period under discussion lies in the fact that it represents the first attempt (aside from those by Marx and Engels themselves, and with the possible exception once again of the Sinological researches of Mad'iar and his students) to test the effectiveness of the Marxist method against a specific body of data, the ground-rules for whose interpretation has been developed in some detail by an international community of scholars. Struve and those who followed his lead may very well have rejected the feudal interpretation of ancient Eastern society partly for political or doctrinal reasons, but once they buttressed this rejection with detailed philological (and, in some later cases, archaeological) arguments, they left the door open for further tests of the theory against empirical evidence. The result was that in time the slaveholding interpretation, which they favored, was also rejected on empirical grounds – although this rejection, to be sure, was not as clear-cut as in the first case.

It should not be thought by any means that Struve's position was accepted immediately or without hesitation. In fact, all of the speakers at the particular session to which the paper that we have been discussing was presented raised more or less serious objections to it. However, again with one exception (the Egyptologist I.M. Lur'e), they are not prepared to defend the feudal interpretation as such. The reader gets the impression that the discussants, except for Lur'e, see the hypothesis suggested by Struve as a promising way out of an embarrassing situation, and would like to accept it, but are at the same time aware of certain serious difficulties, in terms of both logic and Marxist doctrine. In particular, some commentators are puzzled by the fact that in the ancient East, at least during the early period (in contrast to the Greco–Roman situation), slaveholding was usually collective in nature, with slaves belonging, on the one hand, to the state *per se*, or to the crown, and, on the other, to corporations such as temples, rather than to private individuals. This situation creates severe difficulties in the application of the usual kind of Marxist social analysis, which proceeds in terms of classes with opposed interests. The predominantly collective nature of non-Greco-Roman slavery constitutes a sore point even today. As an example of the kind of reaction provoked by the slaveholding interpretation of ancient Eastern society in its original form, let us quote the comment of A.A. Adzhan on Struve's paper:

> In relation to Egypt, Struve said quite clearly that if it was possible to speak of the commune there in the sense of its class differentiation, this was so only to the degree to which the unified commune was contrasted with slaves.

From this it follows that there was no disintegration within the commune – that is, there was no property inequality and no beginning of classes. On this is based the fundamental thesis of the paper – collective slavery and collective ownership of slaves. To me this collective slavery is entirely incomprehensible, for the simple reason that in the paper the concepts of territorial commune, urban commune, temple, and even royal latifundia coincide.

I read the manuscript very attentively, and reached the conclusion that the temple was the center of the territorial commune, but that the property of the temple was owned by the commune as a whole, like the property of the urban communes. In this case, where did the . . . laborers of which Struve speaks, and who were used in these temples [that is, who worked the temple lands], come from? Were these slaves, who during their free time received provisions gratis, or were they persons who had their own land allotments . . . and had to work a definite amount of time in the temples or on the royal estates in the form of corvée labor? In private conversation, Struve admitted that in ancient Mesopotamia, there existed individual land allotments, but he did not explain in his paper the relationship of the labor expended by each individual person in his individual economy, to his labor in the public sector. It turns out that a particular person worked his individual farm, and does not work in the temple estate, but at the same time has his specified share of the income from the exploitation of slaves, which the temple receives. Thus, in place of clear relationships of production, there exists a kind of cluster of completely incomprehensible connections.[9]

Almost alone among the discussants, S.I. Kovalev comes unequivocally to Struve's defence, noting that even if it could be shown that the majority of immediate producers in the ancient East possessed means of production, in the form of land allotments, this would not by itself prove that they were serfs rather than slaves. In support of his contention, he cites the case of the Spartan helots, and inasmuch as this case acquires considerable theoretical importance in the more recent discussion, Kovalev's reasoning deserves to be set forth in some detail. Most ancient Greek writers refer to helots, whether in Sparta or elsewhere in Greece, as slaves. Kovalev wonders whether this was due only to their lack of sophistication in the methodology of social science or to some other cause. He holds that it was due to the fact that the system of exploitation in this case was a collective one, the *polis* (i.e. the collective of slave-owners) exploiting a group of noncitizens, most of whom were slaves. Therefore, there could not be a distinction in principle between slaves and serfs.

> A slave settled on the land remains a slave under the conditions of slaveholding society. A serf separated from the means of production remains a serf under the conditions of feudal society. This is why serfdom in classical antiquity is of course not a social order, as many of us thought and still think. In fact, if it is a social order, then which one is it? A remnant of the past, or an embryo of the future? Obviously it is not a remnant of the past. Although survivals of clan ownership were very strong – appearing, it is true, in a sharply modified class form – in the system of slaveholding relationships, particularly in Sparta, the serf form of exploitation was definitely not a survival of the clan order. This means that it must be an embryo of the future.[10]

However, Kovalev rejects this idea on the basis of everything which is known about feudalism and also on the basis of recent decisions by the Plenum of the Central Committee of the Communist Party of the Soviet Union. I have not

been able to determine so far what these decisions may
have been, or what their relevance to the matter under
discussion was.

In his rebuttal, Struve yields no ground whatever, except
in asking his critics to wait for his fully documented exposition before rejecting his contentions out of hand. He closes
with an extremely revealing capsule history of the evolution of his views on the ancient Eastern social order.

The basic defect in my preceding historical work
resolves to the fact that I became familiar with
Marxist-Leninism in general, and with the
Marxist-Leninist doctrine of social orders, too late.
When I began to familiarize myself with it, I began also
incidentally to study the Soviet literature which was
available on the history of the ancient East and the
history of the ancient world in general. In it I found a
definition of ancient Eastern society as feudal, and
since this definition coincided with the definition of
those bourgeois historians of the ancient East whose
works had been my guide almost since my high-school
days, I adopted this definition without any particular
criticism at the time (at the beginning of 1930) when I
wrote my article on the history of the ancient East for
the *Great Soviet Encyclopedia*, long passages of which
were read by A.I. Tiumenev during his remarks on my
paper. My definition of the immediate producer and
also of the political and juridical superstructure of
ancient Egyptian society in this article coincided
entirely with the definitions given on the one hand by
Maspero, Meyer and Breasted, and on the other, by
those historians who believed that they were basing
themselves on Marxist methodology. I had not at that
time checked this definition by independent analysis of
all the ancient Eastern material available to me . . .
[W]hen I understood that 'in Egypt there existed a

particular social order which we cannot call feudal,'[11] I attempted to identify the mode of production of ancient Egyptian society with the Asiatic mode of production. At that time I saw as immediate producers only the peasants and craftsmen of Egypt, since such was the force and influence of the conceptions which I had received during my university training. I saw no slaves in Egypt, since neither Eduard Meyer nor Maspero nor Breasted had seen them.[12]

Struve further asserts that when he began to study the documents from Babylonia he discovered material with which Western historians such as Meyer and Maspero hadn't dealt at all.

Struve undertakes this piece of intellectual autobiography in order to rebut the reproach, thrown at him by some of the discussants, that he changes his mind too fast. There is in fact a temptation to see these rapid shifts of opinion as responses to political pressure or to shifts in the party line, and there is no doubt that as far as the attitude toward particular historical events in more recent times than those with which Struve and his colleages were dealing, and toward individual historical figures, was concerned, such pressure was applied. However, I think it behooves us to be cautious in formulating any simple kind of 'political' interpretation of the shifts of scholarly opinion relative to the social order of the ancient Eastern countries. For one thing, the rejection of the feudal interpretation appears to have been due to a felt need for ideological consistency, rather than to any political considerations, properly so-called. For another, I.M. Lur'e, who was Struve's major and most outspoken opponent during the discussion with which we have just been dealing, remained faithful to the feudal interpretation for a number of years after this time,[13] and only changed his opinion much later, toward the end of his life.[14] He continued his scholarly activities, and the record does not indicate that he was disciplined in any way. More importantly, however, we should bear in mind that Soviet Marxist scholars at this point were in the process of learning a method of analyzing social phenomena which was new to them and, in fact, altogether new in its application to ancient history. Marx had given only the most general kind of indication with regard to the precapitalist social order, and Engels, whose work was somewhat more detailed, dealt, in *The Origin of the Family, Private Property and the State* and also in *Anti-Dühring*, primarily with the earliest stages of human history and the transition from the primitive–communal social order to class society. In none of Marx's or Engels's work can one find a detailed analysis of the political economy of any precapitalist social order. Under these conditions it is only natural that the study of ancient history in the Soviet Union during the 1920s and 1930s shows a certain intellectual volatility, and is characterized by wide swings of opinion. The views taken, and the methods used, by Soviet historians of the ancient East during the prewar period have been roundly criticized in more recent works of intellectual history,[15] but on the whole the amount and quality of work done along this line at that time is surprising, considering the terms in which the period is described, both in official Soviet and in dissident or emigré sources.

In view of the at least temporary ascendancy of the 'slaveholding interpretation' of ancient Asiatic society during the period with which we are now dealing, it seems ironic that a paper by S.I. Kovalev should have appeared at the same time which calls into serious question the entire empirical basis for the slaveholding social order. It is perhaps not surprising that this paper should have, so to speak, dropped into the void.[16] The significant passage, for our purposes, from Kovalev's monograph runs as follows:

The slaveholding social order outside the sphere of classical antiquity could obviously exist only where the historical conditions were more or less close to those existing in classical society – or in other words, where the communal-clan relationships disintegrated very rapidly, in an extremely saturated environment of intensive foreign trade and inter-communal relationships (between tribes, cities, and state), wars and colonization. There and only there could patriarchal slavery grow into a slaveholding system – that is to say, could the contradictions between slavery and the system of communal-clan relationships develop further. . . . We do not know any other conditions under which this growth is possible, and it would be an idle occupation to think them up out of our heads. The most favorable natural and historical environment for this was the islands and shorelines of highly segmented and differentiated (from the point of view of natural productive forces) inland seas, with a system of convenient water and land routes, and the close proximity of cultured societies on the one hand and backward peoples on the other. *We find such conditions in full measure only in the Mediterranean area, including certain districts immediately adjacent to it, and in particular Mesopotamia.*[17]

Kovalev seems to be saying here that the slaveholding social order as Marx and Engels conceived of it is a specialized phenomenon of limited spatial and temporal distribution, and that particular and quite rare historical and geographical conditions are needed to bring its characteristic contradictions to full expression. It would appear to follow that, if we speak of the slaveholding order as having prevailed in the states of ancient Asia – including pre-Ptolemaic Egypt, Mesopotamia,[18] India, China, and such provincial areas (in a cultural sense) as Mitanni and the

Hittite Empire – where, by and large, the special conditions mentioned by Kovalev did not obtain, this either is true only in an embryonic sense or else requires a considerable stretching of terms. Chief among the special conditions listed by Kovalev as necessary for the full development of the slaveholding order is the presence of a primitive 'barbarian' hinterland within easy reach which can serve as a ready source of slave labor. This requirement derives from the need for constant replenishment of the supply due to the fact that the living conditions of 'classical' slaves interfered with the natural reproduction of their laborpower for two reasons. First, because of the extremely low level of development of the productive forces, slaves were subject to a kind of 'super-exploitation,' involving the appropriation by the slave-owners not only of the surplus product (as is done by the ruling class under any exploitative social order) but of part of the necessary product as well. Second, the practice of housing slaves in barracks, or under barracklike conditions with no possibility of family life, gave their sexual relations a random and episodic character and sharply reduced their birth-rate. All of these factors, taken together, constituted one of the 'major contradictions' of the slaveholding order, which led to its stagnation and eventual breakdown.

Kovalev interprets the historical evidence as indicating that: (1) the relative number of hereditary slaves in the Greco-Roman world was quite small; (2) attempts to breed slaves on the Roman latifundia of the late Republic and early Empire were generally unsuccessful, although there are some apparent exceptions to this; and (3) enslavement of fellow-citizens for debt, while significant as a source of slaves at certain times and places, was generally forbidden by law during the period of fully developed slaveholding society (in Athens after the legislation of Solon, and in Rome from the late Republic onward) and declined in frequency over the course of time. These interpretations (and also some of those mentioned in the preceding paragraph) can easily be challenged, even by someone like myself, who is not a classical historian by training or specialty, and is familiar only with secondary sources, and primary ones in translation. In regard to the sexual life of slaves in particular, Kovalev appears to have generalized on the basis of the kind of behavior which could be expected from nonprimitive modern people under similar conditions – which is hardly a safe procedure. In some cases, indeed, his own evidence seems to speak against him: on the issue of 'super-exploitation' of slaves, for example, he cites the Roman writer on agriculture, Varro, as recommending that only hired laborers, and not slaves, be used for agricultural work where conditions are particularly dangerous or unhealthful, since slaves are too valuable for such use, and represent too heavy an investment.[19] On the other hand, Varro was writing at a time when the supply of slaves from outside the Empire had been almost completely cut off, and their price had skyrocketed; therefore, his seemingly paradoxical recommendation should perhaps be interpreted as an example of the workings of the 'leading contradiction' of the slaveholding order. The recommendation of Cato the Younger, about 150 years earlier and under quite different economic circumstances, was implicitly just the opposite: slaves should simply be 'used up' and new ones bought. The point I am interested in at the moment, however, is that in Kovalev's rendering – which is in strict accordance with Marxist methodology as traditionally understood – the slavery of classical antiquity looks quite different from what is known under the same name elsewhere, even to scholars using the same methodology.

As we shall see later, most of the points made by Kovalev in the paper which I have been analyzing here were repeated in one form or another by the participants in the later (approximately 1952–75) discussion on precapitalist social orders – with the significant exception of Kovalev himself, who was still alive during its first phase – but without any reference to Kovalev's earlier work, and without the (to me) obvious conclusion being drawn that 'classical' slavery, being an aberrant case, is unsuited for use as the basis of a universal or quasi-universal Marxist social order.[20]

Before proceeding to consider the preliminary stage of the revived debate relative to the ancient Asiatic society, which opened at the end of the 1940s, we must deal with two important texts by Struve which indicate where the matter stood at the beginning of the Second World War in terms of both Marxist exegesis and of empirical knowledge. In 1938, Struve presented to an open session held under the auspices of the Institute of Ethnography, Academy of Sciences, USSR, in celebration of the 120th anniversary of Marx's birth, a paper dealing with Marx's views on early class society; it was published some time later.[21] This paper is significant both because of its pivotal position in time, and because it is Struve's one attempt at formal exegesis, and thus sheds some light on his attitude toward the conceptual scheme within which he worked. The paper begins with a sharp attack on the Aziatchiki (from whom, at this point, nothing had been heard in the public record for more than six years) as having hammered a new social order together out of disconnected statements of Marx, including particularly the famous passage in the *Letters on India* in which Marx lists the three major departments of an Oriental government – namely taxation (that is, internal robbery), war (or foreign robbery), and, finally, public works.[22] This statement by Marx, however, carries no historical label, and therefore some supporters of the concept of the Asiatic mode of production have concluded that Asiatic society, in Marx's opinion, underwent no change over the course of history. But this is a definite slander on Marx as a historian.

For Marx, as for Engels, the Oriental societies are not, in terms of the social order [to which they belong], something undifferentiated and monolithic over the whole course of their many centuries of existence. That Asiatic mode of production which Marx viewed as the first and least progressive stage in the development of class society is by no means dominant in the epoch of antiquity, and in the Middle Ages, and in our time. In his fundamental work, Volume I of *Capital*, Marx gives the temporal limits of this peculiar Oriental type of society. He defined it as the ancient Asiatic mode of production, as is clear from his words, so often quoted, to which nevertheless sufficient attention has not been paid: 'In the ancient Asiatic and other ancient modes of production, we find that the conversion of products into commodities and therefore the conversion of men into producers of commodities holds a subordinate place, . . .'[23] If Marx in his preceding work, *Toward a Critique of Political Economy*, names the Asiatic mode of production first as preceding the classical one, we may assume that he even at that time considered this mode of production as characteristic of Asia in ancient times – during an epoch preceding the classic or Greco-Roman world.[24]

It would appear that Struve is here drawing a distinction between the ancient form of Asiatic society and the more modern ones, in order to avoid having to deal in detail with Marx's *Letters on India* and other texts on which the Aziatchiki relied.

One of the mainstays of the feudal, or nonslaveholding, interpretation of ancient Egyptian society (in both its Western and its Soviet versions) has always been the famous account of the building of the pyramids by Herodotus. It should be noted incidentally that for reasons connected with problems of intellectual history, Egypt in a certain sense played the role of model of ancient Eastern society, at a period before those who were not Sinologists by specialty knew much about China. Struve now attacks the 'pyramid builder' problem by way of a long quotation from chapter 13 of *Capital*, incorporating material by the nineteenth-century British political economist Richard Jones – one of Marx's favorite sources. In the passage cited by Marx, Jones contended specifically that the pyramids were constructed by the nonfarming population, which implies (at least in Struve's opinion) a body of full-time slaves, and not peasants working on a *corvée* basis.[25] As was pointed out earlier, Struve had already made and supported similar contentions with regard to the countries of the Fertile Crescent.

Toward the end of his paper Struve introduces, almost casually, an important idea which is to reappear, in modified and elaborated form, in many of the recent writings which relate, in one way or another to the Asiatic mode of production. He writes:

> We see, thus, in ancient Asiatic despotism, a dual form of exploitation in relation to two different social groups. The exaction of 'tribute-taxes' is a form of exploitation of the 'agricultural population' a form which grew up out of the obligations of the mass of people toward the representatives of the old clan elite. Work on the construction of gigantic structures [that is, both religious – pyramids and temples – and having to do with irrigation] is a form of exploitation of the non-agricultural population. . . .
>
> Summarizing all that has been said, we come to the conclusion that according to Marx the second form of exploitation, characteristic of ancient Oriental society, is slaveholding exploitation – exploitation by the slaveholding kings and priests of the 'non-agricultural workers,' who are slaves. This second form of

exploitation – the slaveholding one – is more progressive than the first, namely the exploitation of rural communes. Whereas the first takes its origin from the obligations of the semi-patriarchal order, the second form of exploitation – the exploitation of the 'non-agricultural population' – arose under the conditions of class society in the process of coming into being. The presence of these two forms of exploitation – patriarchal and slaveholding – creates, according to Marx, the specific character of the first class society, which developed in very ancient times in Asia, Egypt, and Italy.[26]

The major source of difficulty in this concept, from the point of view of classical Marxism, lies in the implication that exploitation arose within primeval – which is to say, preclass – society, of which 'patriarchal' or 'patriarchal-clan' society is the final stage. This point has not been lost on more recent critics – not specifically of Struve's own work, but of later scholars who put foward similar ideas. More important, however, is the fact that Struve here anticipates the point elaborated by more recent writers on this problem:

Early-class society, whether of the Oriental or of the Mediterranean type, is characterized by the inclusion in it of large and more or less deformed fragments[27] of primeval society in the form of peasant communities subject to exploitation (often on a collective basis).[28]

It is fairly clear that Struve, while denying the existence of the Asiatic mode of production *per se*, is here making an effort to accommodate the body of facts to which the Aziatchiki – and more recently those who have taken various intermediate positions – usually refer. Significantly, Struve avoids insisting on the slave status of the bulk of the exploited immediate producers in Egypt. And while in his

1934 paper he characterized the immediate producers of the ancient city-states of the Fertile Crescent as slaves – or, to be more accurate, as resembling slaves more than any other category of people – he had retreated some distance from this position a few years later. The same effort at intellectual compromise which I have mentioned is visible in the second edition of his textbook on the history of the ancient East.[29] As one would expect, Struve here avoids the use of the elaborate exegetical apparatus which he set up in the article which we have just been considering, and limits himself to a straightforward recitation of the facts as he sees them. The picture of the ancient Eastern (particularly Mesopotamian) social order which is presented does not differ in essence from the description given of the Asiatic mode of production given by its adherents, or even from that of Oriental despotism as given by Wittfogel: namely, a relatively stagnant form of social development, with absence of private property in the basic means of production (i.e. land), and with the persistence of communal property and various other institutions dating from the primitive–communal period. In chapter 6, dealing with early Mesopotamian society, the social order which immediately succeeded the primitive–communal one in this area is defined as slaveholding, or primitive slaveholding (the absence of a hyphen here makes a subtle but important difference in terms of the rules of Marxist discourse). However:

> Originally the number of slaves was not great. Like the land, they belonged to [that is, were owned by] the commune, which carried on irrigation and agriculture; the members of this commune were bound by a communal form of property. Individually owned slaves were still relatively few in number. . . . The commune-members collectively owned parcels of land. All warriors were peasants and vice versa. . . . Part of

the land was divided into allotments. These allotments were small and varied within the range of several hectares (not more than twenty). Some of these allotments were given out without compensation, and others in return for tribute or tax equal to $^1/_7$ or $^1/_8$ of the harvest. The land owned by the commune was worked by the free people themselves. The cultivation of land under irrigation was so complex a matter that it could be entrusted to a slave only at a higher level of development of the productive forces. The rank-and-file free citizens worked in the communal fields a third of the year, using livestock, a plow, and other means of production issued to them from the temple household. Obviously the bulk of the allotments of the peasants themselves were also worked with the help of communal livestock. For the four months of their work, the free people received food in the form of barley or emmer (an ancient form of wheat), and for the rest of the time they nourished themselves from their allotments. The quantity of produce which they had received for their work on the temple lands was considerably less than what they produced by their labor. Thus, the surplus product came into the hands of the Patesi [local despot] and the nobility. The slaves worked the year around (primarily on the irrigation system).[30]

In other words, the communal peasantry was exploited by an administrative and/or priestly élite, but not on the basis of ownership of the means of production by the latter *as individuals*. The discrepancy between the ancient Eastern social order (whether this be considered slaveholding, feudal, or of some other kind) and the classical or Greco-Roman one as recognized by Marx and Engels, and in fact by the entire European tradition of ancient history, is obvious.

At this point, the onset of the Second World War, followed by the arduous process of recovery from its effects, caused the development of the Soviet–Marxist theory of history to be suspended for a number of years. While scholarly activity did not come to a complete halt, the training of new specialists almost ceased and publication schedules were sharply reduced; the main central journal of ancient history, *Vestnik drevnei istorii*, was suspended between 1941 and 1946, although some attempt was made in the latter year to cover publications and advances in the interim period. In addition to these externally produced factors, there were also more subtle changes in the intellectual climate. To begin with, during the war and in the immediate postwar years the last of the traditional scholars of ancient history (those whose professional training was complete, and their careers fully established, before the Revolution) died off,[31] and their places were taken by others whose thoughts fell naturally, and without strain, into Marxist categories, however these may have been understood. In conclusion, we should note some administrative changes: for example, GAIMK (that is, the State Academy for the History of Material Culture) for whose foundation in the early 1930s N. Ia. Marr was largely responsible, which was staffed mainly by his students, and which bore his name for a time after his death, was reorganized after the war as the Institute of Archaeology under the Academy of Sciences, USSR, and sharply changed the emphasis of its scientific work, engaging almost exclusively in archaeological studies within the Soviet Union. The primary fact to remember, however, is that the contradictory and internally unstable intellectual situation which was created by the ascendancy of the slaveholding interpretation of ancient Eastern society remained unresolved, and hence contained within itself the potential for a fundamental change as soon as external conditions would permit. As we will see in the next section, the beginning of this change, which took a form that the casual observer might not have expected, preceded the end of the Stalin era, once again demonstrating how hazardous are straight-line political interpretations of Soviet intellectual history.

Prelude to the partial revival of the Asiatic mode of production: *ca* 1948–64

It was clear to thoughtful Marxists (including Marx and Engels themselves) almost from the beginning that the slaveholding social order was the weak link in the Marxist theory of history. This is true for several reasons, of both an empirical and a theoretical nature. First, a form of economic behavior (and not merely of domestic life) based in important respects on mass slavery is extremely limited in its distribution, both geographically and histori-cally. It was found in pure form only in the Mediterranean area, and only during the first few centuries before and after the beginning of the Christian era.[32] In fact, it was probably for this reason that Marx originally put forward the concept of the Asiatic mode of production.

In addition to this, the slaveholding social order exhibits certain differences from other social orders which relate to its dynamics – that is, to the mechanism which causes it to change. The usual Marxist assumption is that within each particular social order, the preconditions for a revolu-tionary change, leading to the introduction of new relation-ships of production, are always maturing and developing, and that these new relationships of production are, as it were, 'carried' in each case by a particular class, to whose fundamental economic interests they correspond. This is the class which is mainly responsible for the revolution – its 'hegemon' to use the Russian term. It should be noted that the main oppressed or exploited class in a given social order is not necessarily the revolutionary class. For example, the serf class in feudal society was not generally revolutionary, except in a spontaneous and largely unconscious way; the class which overthrew the feudal social order and established modern capitalist society was that of the urban craftsmen and merchants – the 'bourgeoisie' in the strict sense. A traditional Marxist theorist would probably explain this apparent anomaly by noting that these people were the bearers of a new set of relationships of production, marked by capitalist (or proto-capitalist) private property and wage labor, whereas the serfs were the carriers of relationships of production – the petty landed property and subsistence economy of the independent peasant household – which were already obsolete.[33]

Marxist theorists appear to have had, almost from the beginning, considerable difficulty in deriving the feudal order out of the slaveholding one by any mechanism of this kind – a difficulty which would be both explained and alleviated if it could be assumed that the slaveholding order as Marx and Engels refer to it was, from the point of view of the total Marxist theory of history, an aberrant phenomenon due to special historical or ecological circumstances. If one assumes (as was commonly done by Soviet scholars during the 1930s) that the major class struggle during the slaveholding social order was that between slaves and slaveholders, one must then determine what relationships of production corresponded to the fundamental economic interests of the slaves as a group. Since most slaves in the Greco-Roman world were of foreign origin – basically prisoners of war or their descendants – this question seems unanswerable with respect to them, although it is true that in some places considerable numbers of peasants fell into slave (or slavelike) status as a result of debt. The interests of these people would presumably call for a return to the status of small, independent peasant proprietors engaged in subsistence farming: in other words, their position in terms of the dynamics of revolution would be the same as that of the medieval serf.

The discussion of 'slaveholding society' which took place in the Soviet scholarly community between 1947 and 1964 – and which embodied, with various modifications and differences of emphasis, the consideration set forth above – flowed in two separate but closely related channels. One part of this discussion concerned the dynamics of the slaveholding social order in its classical and generally accepted sense – that is, as exemplified in the highly developed societies of the Mediterranean Basin, marked by the existence of private property and the development of a market economy on at least a limited scale – while the other related to the nature of the society of the pre-Hellenistic Near East, which, taken as a whole, lacked these features. This entire discussion, but particularly the first part, resulted in a loosening of the conceptual structure and a realignment of categories which, in my opinion, has now brought about (or is in the process of bringing about) a fundamental change in the nature of the Soviet Marxist theory of history.

The opening of the discussion was deceptively low-keyed and unobtrusive. In the first issue of the journal *Vestnik drevnei istorii* for 1947 there appeared an editorial entitled 'Toward the Study of the History of the Peasantry in Ancient Times,' which signalled an important change in what might be called the classical early Soviet analysis of slaveholding society, and particularly of the class struggle in societies of this type. The editorialist states:

> The study of ancient slavery [*antichnoe rabstvo*; in other words, that characteristic of classical antiquity]

has not ceased to interest Soviet scholars. However, it would be an unpardonable oversimplification to limit oneself, in studying the economic base of ancient societies, to the analysis of the fundamental antagonism between slaveholders and slaves, and to study the juridical and political superstructure, the civil history, and the intellectual culture of the peoples of antiquity only from this point of view. In classical antiquity we find 'an opposition between the city and the countryside, and later on between states representing urban and rural interests, and within the cities, an opposition between industry and maritime trade.' . . . In the ancient East, the peasants were considered the basic mass of the working population.[34]

In line with this, the editorial points out the basically peasant character of all social movements both in the ancient Near East and in the Greek Golden Age and Hellenistic world – including those movements such as the Maccabean revolt in Palestine, which proceeded under religious or nationalistic slogans. The basic error of Western classical historians who look at Greco-Roman society and the Ancient East, and see capitalism or feudalism (the reference here is obviously to M.I. Rostovtzeff, A.H.M. Jones, and their followers, although they are not mentioned specifically) is that they think in political or juridical terms rather than economic ones. The editorial is written under the very strong influence of Marx's *Pre-Capitalist Economic Formations*, which became available in Russian immediately before the Second World War. This accounts for the added sophistication found here, relative to what was common previously. The effect of the change signalled in this editorial is to downgrade the structural importance of slavery as an element – indeed, the diagnostic element – in the classical social order, by shifting the locus of the major class struggle within it. This in fact is not a totally

new idea in Soviet scholarship: as we have seen, the point
had been made by S.I. Kovalev some thirteen years previously. However, in view of the inaccessibility of Kovalev's
paper, the point made in the editorial has the force of a new
departure.

The next stage in the development of the debate on the
slaveholding social order – and indirectly on the Asiatic
mode of production as well – is represented by another
editorial which appeared in the first issue for 1952; this
editorial deals with the multi-volume series *World History*,
prepared by the Academy of Sciences, USSR. The
editorialist distinguishes two separate stages of slaveholding social order, with different characteristics: the first,
early, or primitive stage (although these terms should not
be taken as necessarily implying a chronological difference) is marked by

> a patriarchal[35] system of slavery directed toward the
> production of the immediate means to life, and not of
> commodities; a weak development of
> commodity-and-money relationships; debt slavery; the
> presence of a significant class of petty producers –
> primarily peasants who have not been driven off the
> land; an Oriental[36] form of property; a form of state
> and of culture corresponding to the designated social
> order (despotism, a slow pace of cultural development,
> etc.).

The second or fully developed stage of slaveholding society
is characterized by

> a higher development of the productive forces; a system
> of slavery directed toward the production of
> commodities, the displacement of free labor by slave
> labor in the basic spheres of production; the
> pauperization of the petty producers as a result of this;
> the elimination of debt slavery; the numerical

predominance of privately-owned slaves over other
categories; the classical [Greco-Roman] form of
property and the forms of state and culture
corresponding to this social order (the *polis* in its
highest form . . .).[37]

If we compare these quotations with what was said previously, it is fairly clear that early slaveholding society, as
defined here, corresponds roughly to the social order based
on the Asiatic mode of production – even though certain
elements of it are absent or appear in veiled form. There is,
for example, no mention of the role of irrigation, or of
ultimate state ownership of the land – unless, indeed, this is
covered by the ambiguous phrase 'Oriental form of property.' By the same token, the developed stage of slaveholding society corresponds to the Greco-Roman social order
as it was identified by Marx and Engels, and in the Western
historical tradition generally. Here also the description
given by the editorialist gives some elements which the
facts do not warrant: for example, independent peasant
populations were not completely driven off the land or
pauperized even in the late Roman Empire. In that sense,
the position taken in this editorial marks a retreat from that
of the 1947 editorialist, and even from that of Kovalev in
1934, both of whom emphasize the social role of the
peasantry in the classical world.

The subsequent discussion, mostly in the pages of *Vestnik drevnei istorii*, but later including articles in some other
journals, proceeds along two separate lines, only one of
which will be dealt with in any detail here. In the first place,
Soviet classical historians – chiefly those concerned with
later antiquity – tried to resolve some of the contradictions
inherent in the concept of the slaveholding social order as it
existed at the time, particularly in terms of its 'laws of
motion.'[38] The most troublesome of these contradictions
relates to the transition from the slaveholding social order

to feudalism, and particularly to the character of the major social disturbances of late Imperial times, which turn out to have been, not slave revolts at all, but basically peasant uprisings. Normally – on the analogy of the bourgeois and socialist revolutions – one would expect the ruling class of the future social order to be the main agent in the revolution leading to that order. In this case, however, we apparently have the oppressed class of the feudal social order which is in process of formation – that is, the peasantry – fighting for the ascendancy of this order, and the future ruling class of large landowners fighting against it. Shtaerman[39] puts it this way:

> In essence, all those who struggled against the state in
> the late Empire were struggling against relationships
> arising from the slaveholding order, which had already
> decayed. However opposed the interests of the
> feudalizing landowners and the farmers in the process
> of being enserfed may have been, and however
> different the causes may have been which drove one or
> another to ally themselves with people from outside the
> Empire, their actions in the final analysis led to
> identical results, namely to the establishment of a new
> political form, and ultimately to the reinforcement of
> elements of feudalism. This is explained by the fact that
> both of these classes were classes of the feudal order in
> process of formation, for whose development the
> liquidation of the survivals of slavery was required.
> However, the mass of dependent and enserfed farmers
> of various categories did desire the most complete
> liquidation of these survivals and the division of the
> land, which would yield the easiest and surest path to
> the new development of the new relationships; on the
> other hand, the landowning elite strove for the
> preservation of all those survivals of the previous order
> which could facilitate the reinforcement of its power

over the immediate producer, and which would hinder the development of the new order and make it more trying for the masses.

The position taken here is criticized from various angles by Kazhdan and Korsunskii, and most significantly by Kovalev,[40] who concluded that the social revolution of the late Empire was a revolution of an essentially different type from those of later times – completely destructive, having no hegemonic class, and leading to the downfall of the existing, slaveholding social order, but not to the ascendancy of its successor. In reaching this conclusion, Kovalev tries to show that even this destructive social revolution was called forth by a disjunction between the productive forces (that is, the state of the technology) and the relationships of production, and therefore conforms to the pattern originally hypothesized by Marx. This represents a complex problem which cannot be gone into here; I will merely give it as my personal opinion that this is the weakest link in the Marxist theory of history as it relates to precapitalist periods; the technological advance as between late antiquity and early feudalism simply does not seem sufficient to account by itself for the major change in the relationships of production which took place.

By the end of the 1950s, it was obvious that, if the use of the concept of the slaveholding social order involved such serious difficulties even in the interpretation of social relations in classical antiquity proper, this concept was still less suited for the handling of data from the ancient Near East. The intellectual situation in this area is rather curious in several respects. From the end of the Second World War until 1964, no Soviet scholar, to my knowledge, refers to the social order of the ancient Near East as anything other than slaveholding, although some attach a qualifying adjective – 'early,' or 'primitive,' or 'undeveloped' – to this designation, usually omitting the hyphen. At the same time, a very large volume of material appeared, both in *Vestnik drevnei istorii* and in separate books, which made it quite obvious that the social order in question differed sharply from that of classical antiquity even in the earliest stages of the latter – say, the type of society reflected in the Homeric poems. The authors of this material included not only the scholars who had opposed Struve's interpretation since it was first advanced during the 1930s – such as I.M. Lur'e – and those who were inclined to argue with him on particular philological or methodological issues – such as I.M. D'iakonov and A.I. Tiumenev – but also, and to no small extent, Struve himself.[41]

Thus in the latter half of the 1950s, the slaveholding interpretation of ancient Eastern society was progressively undermined without being formally repudiated. At the end of the period under discussion here, the stage was set for an attempt at formal revival of the concept of the Asian mode of production. The culminating stages in this process are represented by A.I. Tiumenev's 1967 two-part article, 'The Near East and Classical Antiquity,'[42] and by I.M. D'iakonov's important paper, 'The Commune in the Ancient East as Treated in the Works of Soviet Researchers,' together with the record of the oral discussion to which it gave rise.[43] It must not be thought that either Tiumenev or D'iakonov in these articles took an 'Aziatchik' position. Rather, they seem to have been concerned to defend the concept of the slaveholding social order generally (not necessarily as applied to ancient Eastern society) against those who either interpreted the concept too narrowly or, in the authors' opinion, misread the historical evidence. The particular importance of Tiumenev's paper lies in the fact that it: (1) spelled out, more clearly than had been done up to that point, the empirical differences between the social order of the ancient Near East (including Egypt, Mesopotamia, and pre-Hellenistic Asia Minor) and that of classical antiquity

in the Mediterranean area; and (2) for the first time suggested explicitly that these two social orders were not
temporally distinct forms of the same phenomenon (as is
implied to varying degrees by the use of the terms 'early/
primitive/undeveloped slaveholding,' with or without the
hyphen) but two social orders, distinct in terms of their
laws of motion and of equal conceptual status.[44] It is traditional in Marxist discourse to limit the concept of 'fully
developed slaveholding society' to situations where the
bulk of the exploited persons are members of ethnically
alien groups and/or prisoners of war and their children. It
was precisely on this basis that Eastern society was
declared (by Struve and a number of other authors of
standard Soviet textbooks on ancient history) to be characterized by an immature form of slaveholding. This limitation of the concept of slaveholding of course flows out of –
or, to put it another way, presupposes – a sharp conceptual
distinction between slave and free status, such as actually
existed, for example, in Periclean Athens or the Roman
Republic. Tiumenev mounts a frontal attack on this idea, in
the course of which he extends the category of 'slave' to
almost the entire population of the despotic states of the
ancient East. The corollary of this is of course that, where
everyone is a slave (except perhaps the ruler) no one is a
slave in any real sense. A critic, working at twenty years'
temporal distance, and at a spatial distance of half the
circumference of the world from the original author, is
tempted to conclude that Tiumenev was here striving to
retain the verbal form of the concept of slaveholding society, while completely changing its content. There seems to
be no doubt that this was the actual effect of his article. As I
have already suggested, and will show in more detail later
on, some Soviet scholars have now concluded, with varying
degrees of certainty, that the 'classical social order' – which
is to say, that of the Greco-Roman world – was an aberration due to the particular geographical and climatic condi-

tions, which owes its salient positions in Marxist thought to its extraordinary importance in the context specifically of Western history.

The paper by D'iakonov cited in note 43 represents a considerable intellectual advance over Tiumenev's work, just discussed, in that it offers a specific theory to account for the comparatively limited importance of slavery in the strict sense in the societies of the Fertile Crescent and of Pharaonic Egypt, which are traditionally designated as slaveholding societies in Marxist historical scholarship. The terms in which D'iakonov presents this theory deserve to be quoted at length, since their importance cannot be overestimated.

Often, in our attempts to find slavery in a particular ancient society (efforts which are sometimes in vain), we have not given thought either to the question of whether slave labor would have been economically advantageous under the particular conditions we are studying, or whether the particular society possessed sufficient means of compulsion to make the mass employment of slave labor possible. For example, in the early Sumerian city-states, where the standard means of compulsion consisted merely of the small group of the rulers' henchmen, armed with copper axes and having no armor, it was impossible to employ slaves in . . . field tasks requiring large numbers of hands. *This was so not because the society had not matured to the point of the creation of surplus products by slave labor, but because the mass of former soldiers, now slaves with copper hoes in their hands, could not physically be compelled to work in the fields, and it was dangerous to attempt to compel them.* Therefore, for a long period, it was preferred to kill male prisoners and to employ the labor of slave women and their children in the home, under supervision and in crafts, thereby

freeing the labor of free persons for field work. . . .
Slave labor in *agricultural* production should not
necessarily be considered characteristic of the first type
of class system . . . which we call the slave-owning
system of production. With the exception of certain
special cases, the use of slaves for agriculture becomes
possible only when the slave system is well advanced.
On the other hand, in places where the goal of
production was not the mass-scale output of
commodities (and this was the case in the majority of
ancient societies), slave production, requiring not only
that the resistance of the enslaved be overcome but that
capital – not immediately recoverable – be invested for
the acquisition of slaves whose productivity was lower
than that of free workers, did not always prove to be
economically more advantageous. Therefore, no
ancient society ever attained, or could attain, the
complete replacement of free labor by slave labor.
Alongside slave production, there always existed
small-scale subsistence production by independent free
producers.[45]

The explanation offered by D'iakonov for the limited
importance (both quantitatively and structurally) of true
slavery in the societies with which he was dealing – namely,
the absence of adequate means of compulsion – was quite
compatible with the Marxist intellectual tradition. That is
to say that D'iakonov here provided the basis upon which a
new social order, which would be neither slaveholding nor
feudal, could be set up – although, as the alert reader will
notice, he does not take the next step of actually hypostasizing and naming this social order. It can be said that the
central issue of the Marxist interpretation of ancient Eastern society is here faced squarely for the first time since the
debates of the early 1930s, which were dealt with in part
one of the present volume.

74

However, D'iakonov has not succeeded in sweeping aside at one stroke all the intellectual difficulties in this area. If one assumes that the society of the Sumerian city-states, and its successor societies in the same general area, were *antagonistic* societies – which is to say, were marked by exploitative relationships – the question then remains: what part of the population was exploited, and how was this exploitation carried out, in the absence of armament sufficient to compel slaves equipped with hoes to work in the fields? One would think that a technology sufficient to permit the development of the state – even in its most primitive form – with its characteristic means of compulsion for extracting taxes from the population (and this structure certainly existed in the Fertile Crescent from a very ancient date) would also permit the exploitation of slave labor. The issues relating to the fundamental character of ancient Eastern society and to the nature and direction of exploitation within it were not addressed squarely by the participants in the discussion of D'iakonov's paper, which was perhaps not surprising in view of the fact that an entire field was being opened up for discussion in explicit terms for the first time in at least thirty years. It seems clear, however, that the discussants – or at least some of them – were aware that the 'slaveholding interpretation' of ancient Eastern society was being fundamentally challenged. In his remarks at the end of the discussion, D'iakonov asserted that 'exploitation did exist – not of the commune as a whole or of members of the commune as such, but only of a particular portion of the members. Taxes in themselves are not a sign of exploitation. "Even Rockefeller pays taxes,". . .'[46] This, of course, is an implicitly anti-Aziatchik position, since one of the salient features of the Asiatic mode of production, according to its proponents, is the use of taxation as the major mode of exploitation, or the coincidence between rent and taxes. A more correct formulation, from the point of view

75

of traditional Marxism, would have been that whether or not taxation constitutes exploitation, relative to any particular individual or group, depends on who is in control of the state machinery at the time in question.

At a later point, the summary of D'iakonov's concluding remarks indicates that he would like to restrict the concept of exploitation of the commune as a whole or of its members *per se* to situations existing at much later periods, when

> the richer and higher-born members of the commune did not themselves perform duties, and sometimes did not pay taxes, but sent their poor kinsmen, debtors or slaves, to do so. They continued to be considered members of the commune and enjoy the right of citizenship offered by the commune, but this already provides the foundation for a situation in which the topmost stratum is separated out to the commune, and the members of the commune begin to be subjected to exploitation. This is one of the forms of gradual dissolution of the archaic primitive mass of free members of the commune, from both ends at once, into two antagonistic classes. . . . It is no accident, D'iakonov emphasized, that all who uphold the idea that 'the commune was exploited' cite late material. This is true of the Han dynasty in China, the late Assyrian period, late Babylonia, the Seleucid Empire, etc.[47]

This formulation, while it cannot, perhaps, be faulted as a reading of the historical evidence, leaves an unsatisfactory intellectual situation in terms of formal Marxism, since, for the earlier period (before the commune presumably began to break down) we have the state – by definition an organ of class domination – existing under conditions where there was no clearly defined exploited class. As we shall see in what follows, this point was not lost on the later participants in the discussion.

The revival of the Asiatic mode of production

After the publication of D'iakonov's paper on the commune, and of the record of the discussion on it, the 'slaveholding interpretation' of ancient Eastern society was no longer maintained in the form which had become traditional. During the Seventh International Congress of Anthropological and Ethnographic Sciences, held in Moscow during August 1964, papers by the French Marxist scholars Jean Suret-Canale and Maurice Godelier, dealing explicitly with the concept of the Asian mode of production, were circulated in manuscript form, along with a response by Academician V.V. Struve, even though the authors were not physically present. I have not been able to discover who did the circulating or under what circumstances, but in any case this circulating had the effect of reintroducing the Asian mode of production, *under that name*, into Soviet discourse. Abstracts of the apparently unpublished papers by Suret-Canale and Godelier, together with the complete (though relatively brief) paper by Struve, were almost immediately published in the journal *Narody Azii i Afriki* (Peoples of Asia and Africa).[48]

It must have been rather hard for the Soviet reader – unless, indeed, he or she had been a witness of the earlier discussions or had read the record of them (which was theoretically possible, since the necessary books exist in some libraries in the USA, and presumably in the Soviet Union as well) – to make out from the abstracts by the French scholars just what points were at issue, but Struve's

77

reply is clear enough in most respects and quite surprising on a number of counts. He raises no objection in principle to the use of the concept of the Asiatic mode of production, and in fact seems to take it as a matter of standard Marxist practice.[49] Struve here seems mainly concerned to combat the revisionist implications of the position taken by the French scholars – implications which, by the way, are not visible from the published abstracts. Struve's stance throughout the article is that of a Marxist fundamentalist, although it is significant that this piece (like most of his other writings, and unlike much of the other material which had appeared during the earlier period) is quite unpolemical in tone.

Struve accuses Godelier of unwitting adherence to a cyclical model of the historical process, because the latter admits the possibility of several paths of development running from the decay of the primitive–communal order up to incipient capitalism, all of these paths being of equal status. In the context of 'official Marxism' at that time, Godelier's position no doubt was deviationist, and it may even have been so relative to Marx's own work (although this is a separate question, not directly dealt with in the present paper). However, within less than two years from the formal reopening of the discussion on the Asiatic mode of production, a spate of discussion articles proposing various models of historical development for various parts of the world was appearing in the Soviet scholarly press,[50] and it seemed as though the Marxist theory of history, in its Soviet version, was in process of fundamental transformation.[51] I should emphasize once more that this reversal of intellectual field was not as abrupt in terms of substance as the linguistic form which it took made it appear. It had been clear for quite a while that the three-stage sequence of antagonistic societies (slaveholding–feudal–capitalist) could no longer be maintained in its old form, even apart from the special problems raised by the riverine 'hydraulic' empires of the ancient Near East (including Egypt). Even those entrusted with the fairly modest tasks of writing informational articles and compiling records of oral discussions make this point without compromise.[52] At the same time, the importance of the change in terms of verbal form should not be underestimated. By explicitly reviving the concept (and the expression) 'Asiatic mode of production,' which had been originated by Marx – rather than simply describing the state of affairs to which it referred, as Struve and others had been doing for some time – the participants in the discussion of the early and middle 1960s fundamentally changed the character and the parameters of Marxist debate, as it occurred in the Soviet context.

During the later 1960s and early 1970s, a considerable body of material relating in one way or another to the question of the Asiatic mode of production – or, more broadly, to the question of the criteria for distinguishing between the various precapitalist social orders – continued to appear in the Soviet scholarly press, and elaborate oral debates on the topic became a regular feature of academic life. All of this certainly indicated not only intense interest in matters relating to the Marxist theory of history in a large part of the intellectual public, but also some sense of urgency in regard to these matters on the part of those who considered it their function to supervise and guide Soviet intellectual life. Unfortunately, I am not in a position to state with any precision what the social and political grounds of this urgency were. It should however be noted that one of the most striking characteristics of the more recent debate is the persistence of general points of view, and even in some cases of individual arguments, from the earlier one.

On 27 and 28 May 1965, a special discussion was held under the auspices of the Academic Council of the Institute of the Peoples of Asia, Academy of Sciences, USSR (Moscow branch), on the topic 'Common Elements and

Peculiarities in the Historical Development of Peoples of the East.' The record of this discussion was later published in a book with the same title under the editorship of a committee headed by G.F. Kim (see note 52, first item). Some of the participants revived and expanded their remarks for publication; in other cases, the remarks were published according to the stenographic transcript of the discussion.

This discussion marked the official reopening of the debate on the Asiatic mode of production in the Soviet Union – that is, in a sense of an actual, flesh-and-blood event, rather than merely the publication of journal articles and books. The introductory address was given by Kim who immediately made clear the ideological auspices under which the discussion was being held, and the limits to which it would be subject.

> Many bourgeois sociologists of this [anti-Marxist] tendency declare Marxism to be 'inapplicable' to countries with a predominantly peasant population. They exaggerate the thesis as to the exceptional nature of the historical development of the countries of the East and hence as to the complete inapplicability to them of the 'European model' (i.e., the general laws of history). By so doing, these sociologists, fulfilling a particular assignment,[53] strive to expand the nutrient medium for the ultra-nationalist elements which at times try for egoistic reasons to establish a 'special path' for Eastern people and an exceptional role in world history for them, and split the unity of the anti-imperialist forces, opposing peoples to each other along racial and national lines. . . . In their attempts to validate 'in a new way' the role of social classes in history, they lay special emphasis on the stability of the patriarchal commune in the countries of the East, trying to show that this factor is decisive even in our times. It

is not hard to notice that behind this there is concealed
a persistent effort to 'idealize' the peasantry and to
present it as a leading factor in historical development,
regardless of periods or socio-economic orders.[54]

Kim here points out the explicitly political dangers inherent in the theory of the Asiatic mode of production – or
perhaps we had better say, in any undue recognition of the
distinctive nature of the social order characteristic of the
ancient East. It is interesting that these dangers are seen (in
the second part of the quotation, following the ellipsis) in
explicitly 'exceptionalist' terms,[55] even though, to the best
of my knowledge the social order of imperial China is
defined by Chinese Communist scholars as a feudal one.

The main paper by V.N. Nikiforov, 'The Conception of
the Asiatic Mode of Production and Current Soviet Historiography' ('Kontseptsiia aziatskogo sposoba proizvodstva i sovremennaia sovetskaia istoriografiia'), which
forms the basis of the discussion proper, sets forth what
might be called a moderate or liberal anti-Aziatchik position. That is to say, it repeats the arguments against accepting the concept of the Asiatic mode of production as part of
a Marxist arsenal which were marshalled during the
debates of the early 1930s, but strips them of the political
invectives which were common at that time. In fact
Nikiforov specifically expresses sympathy with early Soviet
scholars such as E.S. Varga who, he admits, were unjustly
vilified because of their adherence to the Aziatchik position. Nikiforov points out quite accurately that no
Aziatchik, either Soviet or foreign, had yet been able to
demonstrate conclusively the presence of the Asiatic mode
of production in any concrete society. He devotes a long
passage toward the beginning of his paper to a detailed
critique of Ter-Akopian's two-part article (see part one of
the present monograph, especially note 6) which concludes
by unequivocally declaring Marx and Engels to have been

Aziatchiki. Nikiforov makes some headway on this front, mainly through a careful analysis of Engels's *Origin of the Family, Private Property and State*, which makes no mention of the Asiatic mode of production and whose importance Ter-Akopian discounts. However, the positive portions of Nikiforov's paper are not marked by particular clarity of thought or cogency of expression. For example, in discussing the social order characteristic of ancient China, as it can be reconstructed from the data collected by current Soviet Sinologists, he remarks: 'This is not feudalism, inasmuch as the prevailing form of compulsion is not economic, not based on feudal land tenure; on the contrary, land is still plentiful and little valued. But this is also not the Asiatic system; there exist private ownership of the means of production and . . . a ruling class of private owners.'[56]

In the context of the Marxist tradition as a whole, the first part of the statement has a strange sound. In the first place, feudalism – like any precapitalist antagonistic social order – is marked precisely by *non*economic compulsion. In the second place, it is not clear what difference the land-supply makes in terms of the existing social order, although, on a common-sense basis, one could probably say that it would be difficult to 'attach' people permanently to the land under conditions where vacant land was available to anyone who took the trouble to settle and cultivate it. Nikiforov emphasizes in every possible way the presence of private property in the means of production of those societies which have been described by some Soviet scholars as being marked by the Asiatic mode of production. His paper is part of an obvious attempt by the organizers of the discussion to limit the intellectual appeal and significance of the concept of the Asiatic mode of production and to discredit this concept as a tool of Marxist analysis – but without resorting to the crudely anti-intellectual methods characteristic of the first debate in its closing stages. However, this attempt is not notably successful: it founders on the theoretical problems and difficulties inherent in the concept of the social order which is traditional in Marxism. Indeed, Nikiforov recognizes that much in the closing sentence of his paper.[57]

The printed comments of the discussants yield a highly variegated, if not chaotic picture of the situation of Soviet Oriental studies at this time. The discussions include a small group of 'stand-patters' who favor the retention of the traditional five-step (or three-step, if primitive–communal society and socialist society are omitted) model of social development unchanged: A.G. Krymov, M.A. Korostovtsev, K.Z. Ashrafian, and S.M. Dubrovskii. They also include an even smaller group of what might be called modified or neo-Aziatchiki: L.A. Sedov, V.V. Krylov and a few others who share their views in differing degrees. I refer to these people as 'modified' Aziatchiki because, while they recognize the existence of a social order based on relatively independent rural communes dominated and exploited through taxation by a despotic, bureaucratic regime, where private property in the means of production was either absent or rudimentary, they do not regard this social order as a universal stage in human history, as would be required by a literal interpretation of Marx's original listing. The remainder of the discussants cannot be easily classified on either side of the debate in terms of its earlier version, although some of them propose solutions to the theoretical problems relating to the slaveholding social order which are hardly less radical than the most extreme Aziatchik position. For example, Iu. M. Kobishchanov, contending that throughout the period of classical antiquity the main exploited group was that of the 'petty producers' – nominally independent subsistence peasants – opts for the complete scrapping of the slaveholding social order, and a definition of the social order of classical antiquity in terms of various types and phases of feudalism.[58] In general, it could be said that even those who specifically reject the Asiatic mode of production as a concept and an analytical tool do not defend the original three-step model for the development of class society – unless, like Kim and to some extent Nikiforov, they are specifically playing political rather than scholarly roles.

The discussion which I have just summarized was continued or resumed in 1971, but in written rather than oral form, and by, so to speak, a rump session.[59] The contributors are Nikiforov, Krymov and G.F. Il'in, along with I.M. D'iakonov and Iu. V. Kachanovskii, who did not take part in the original discussion. Because of the small number of contributors, the greater congruence of their views, and the greater formality and length and fuller documentation of their papers, this collection gives a rather different impression of the intellectual situation than the reader is likely to receive from the 1966 volume. However, this difference seems to me to some extent superficial. The points made in criticism of the theory of the Asiatic mode of production, in its original form (which at the time of this publication was at least forty years old), are in some cases quite telling if not very original; with the exception of Kachanovskii, who is dealing specifically with the view and arguments of Western European Marxists on the topic, the contributors merely repeat the earlier criticisms. On the positive side, they find themselves obliged – particularly in the case of D'iakonov – to perform considerable intellectual gymnastics in order to sustain a traditional sequence of social orders, in which the fatally flawed (at least according to my interpretation of the Marxist method) concept of the slaveholding mode of production must play a central role. However, this second collection does include certain intellectual advances over these earlier works, and does make explicit certain matters which were only hinted at previously.

The opening paper by Nikiforov, 'Marx and Engels on

the Asiatic Mode of Production' ('K. Marks i F. Engel's ob aziatskom sposobe proizvodstva') is essentially an expanded and cleaned-up version of the main paper for the 1966 discussion. The surface confusions and ambiguities, such as the one mentioned earlier concerning the nature of compulsion under the feudal system, have been removed; the deeper questions remain. The chain of argument is too detailed and scholastic to be summarized here, but in the final section we have for the first time a consistent and fully formed position on the twin questions: Why did Marx include the Asiatic mode of production in his original sequence of social orders? And why is this sequence in its original form not now binding on those who consider themselves Marxists? This position can be summarized as follows.

At one stage of his career, culminating in the late 1850s with the introduction to *Toward a Critique of Political Economy* and *Pre-Capitalist Economic Formations*, Marx actually was an Aziatchik; all attempts to prove otherwise are artificial and invalid.

Marx at that time hypothesized a special Asiatic mode of production with certain specific characteristics (organization of the population into communes, despotic-bureaucratic character of the state, importance of public works and particularly hydraulic installations, absence or undeveloped character of private property in land) on the basis of accounts by Western travellers and colonial administrators describing Indian, and, in a few cases, Chinese society – accounts which suffered from the unconscious cultural biases of their authors, who were unable to find private property of the familiar Western bourgeois type and therefore concluded that no private property of any kind existed in the Oriental societies which they observed.

The hypothesis of the Asiatic mode of production as a 'full member' of the sequence of social orders is not characteristic of mature Marxian[60] thought; it was gradually abandoned by Marx under the impact of later and more accurate data, and is not found as such either in *Anti-Dühring* or in *The Origin of the Family, Private Property and the State*.

Any revival of the concept of the Asiatic mode of production at the present point in intellectual history must depend on data and considerations of which Marx and Engels were not aware.[61]

The important point to be noted here is that according to the formulation the politically 'orthodox' anti-Aziatchik position proves to be revisionist in terms of doctrine – based on a kind of Marxist 'higher criticism' – while the Aziatchiki (politically revisionist in the opinion of Iolk, Zorkii, Dubrovskii and other participants in the earlier debates, and also implicitly in that of Kim) are depicted as Marxist fundamentalists, who cite Marx and Engels like Scripture, in a fashion which is essentially ahistorical in respect of the development of their thought. The major change which causes this point to emerge fully is Nikiforov's abandonment of any attempt to make Marx's original sequence of social orders 'inoperative' on a textual or exegetical basis – that is, by changing the translation of the text or by showing that the author somehow did not mean what he appears to have written *at the time he wrote it* – as Iolk and Dubrovskii tried to do forty years previously. The attentive reader will remember that Godes argued somewhat along the same lines in the 1929 debate, but his viewpoint did not prevail at the time. It remains to be seen, of course, what the ultimate success of Nikiforov's adventure will be, but as we will see in a moment, other and still more radical proposals have appeared since the publication of his article, and indeed some were already in print before then.

Iu. V. Kachanovskii's contribution to this collection, 'Diskussiia ob aziatskom sposobe proizvodstva na stranitsakh zarubezhnoi marksistskoi pechati' ('The Discussion on the Asiatic Mode of Production in the Foreign Marxist Press') deals with non-Soviet (and mainly Western European) literature, and thus falls for the most part outside the scope of this monograph. However, Kachanovskii's general conclusion is of some importance, and is, in my opinion, largely justified. He holds that, judged by the criteria usually applied to scientific hypotheses – the capacity to grow and develop, to be tested against reality, and to generate new insights – the theory of the Asiatic mode of production is a failure.

It has remained in approximately the original form in which it was advanced in 1964 by the journal *La Pensée*. Furthermore, no hypotheses have been advanced which would open up the road to the clarification of the nature and profound regularities of the Asiatic mode of production. The more the discussion has developed, the more obvious it has become that about the character of the Asiatic mode of production there was nothing more to say. Apparently for this reason, in the past few years a quite obvious turn has become evident: the conception of the Asiatic mode of production is increasingly receding into the background and questions of the general history of pre-capitalist societies are occupying the center of attention.[62]

Whatever might be the response of non-Soviet Marxists to this judgment, it is significant that it is not made on explicitly political grounds, or even on ideological ones – as similar judgments have been made in the past – but in a way which presupposes that the Marxist theory of history as a whole and its component parts (real or purported, necessary or superfluous) stand or fall on their explanatory power with respect to actual historical facts. The intellectual genie has been let out of the bottle, and even if someone wants to put him back in, this may prove to involve unanticipated difficulties.

The recent argumentation by I.M. D'iakonov on the social structure of ancient Oriental society, both in his contribution to the volume which I am now discussing ('The Basic Features of Ancient Society: A Summary based on Data from Western Asia' ('Osnovnye cherty drevnego obshchestva: referat na materiale Zapadnoi Azii')) and in a slightly later paper which is in part a revision of this one,[63] is of the greatest possible interest; it amounts to an extremely subtle and sophisticated defence of the 'slaveholding interpretation' of ancient Oriental society, of a kind which, if generally accepted, will contribute to a fundamental change in the character of the Marxist theory with which the second part of the present monograph is chiefly concerned.

As the following analysis will show, D'iakonov's argument, while on the whole promising and superior in intellectual grasp and cogency to competing formulations such as Melikishvili's,[64] is marred at some points by scholasticism and straining of terms, and raises certain potentially severe problems in terms of future development.

D'iakonov is concerned first of all to combat what he takes to be a widespread misconception to the effect that private ownership of the means of production (chiefly land) was virtually nonexistent in the kingdoms of the ancient Near East. Although the jurisprudence of that time and place had not yet arrived at a clear distinction between the functions of the ruler in private and in public law – that is, between his rights and privileges as a ruler and as owner of real property – the juridical documents show beyond question that any ruler or state could sell its land and still retain its political sovereignty over that land, or could buy land from its subjects without the political status of that land changing in any way. Therefore, one of the important criteria for the existence of the Asiatic mode of production proves to be based on a false assumption. D'iakonov divides all land and property in the kingdoms of the ancient Near East into two basic categories: first, that of the state; and second, that of communes – which he calls private property in the sense that it did not belong to the state.[65]

The evolution of both of these sectors is of considerable interest. The original task of the state economic operations (in Mesopotamia, in the Fourth and the first half of the Third Millennia B.C.E.) was the creation of a fund of goods for insurance and exchange; from the end of the Third Millennium B.C.E., these operations are transformed into a source of income for the king and the royal bureaucracy. Later, after the fall of the Third Dynasty of Ur (approximately 2,000 B.C.E), the state operations as such are continually reduced, and that part of the state's land fund which is set apart for the maintenance of royal functionaries, warriors, and craftsmen, by payment in kind, grows. Thus, in the Second Millennium B.C.E., there also arise in the state sector what are in effect private farms – but the possessors and tenants of these farms are not their owners.[66]

At this point, D'iakonov confronts directly the question of the social structure of ancient Near East society – into what categories the population was divided, which of these were exploited, and who did the exploiting – which is the central question when it comes to determining to what social order a particular society belongs. D'iakonov's reasoning here is at once the most interesting and the trickiest aspect of his argument.

The languages of the ancient Near East show that the population was divided in two major ways. The first of these divisions was between persons having authority and persons living under authority. A person having authority might be either the ruler in his or her own right, in relation to the economic operations belonging to the state, or else the patriarch of a joint family – a person who managed the land belonging to that unit as an administrator or custodian. Persons living under authority, in relation to the ruler, were all those who held land or other material goods from the ruler not by ownership but on condition of service – functionaries, warriors, craftsmen, and the working personnel of the royal economic operations, and in a certain sense all the subjects. Those living under authority in relation to the patriarch of a joint family in the 'private' (communal) sector were all those persons who received and used supplies or material goods within the limits of the family economy, but did not participate in its ownership – that is, minor sons and other junior kinsmen, clients, debtors, and slaves.

> This is the simplest of the divisions which existed. But it is oversimplified, even from the point of view of the ancients, since people who were not property-owners and persons subject to the authority of the ruler can by no means, alas, be equated with minor children or slaves; neither can adult persons, who actually had their own farms and people under their own authority.
> Hence the second division – the famous Babylonian division of society (excluding slaves) into *avilum* and *muškenum*: that is into people who although adults in both cases were property owners in the first case (*avilum*), but not in the second (*muškenum*).
> Incidentally, we should make the qualification that as the result of the purchase of land not held on condition of service – that is, land belonging solely to communes – by the elite of the royal functionaries, and in general as the result of the process of social fusion of the elite of the ruler's people with the commune members, the term *avilum* begins to be used in relation to the elite, and *muškenum* only in relation to the more or less deprived royal farmers and other 'bringers of income,'

90

as the Babylonian phrase had it. However, the actual, objective class division was a different one.[67]

D'iakonov lists as follows the categories of persons who were exploited: first, slaves, but until the Third and Second Millennia BCE, chiefly slave women because of the lack of reliable means of compulsion to protect the slave-owner against the rebellion of the legal slaves; second, people in a patriarchally dependent position, such as younger kinsmen and clients; third, debtors; and fourth, royal workers or state helots. This last group of people was exploited by a combination of means, and in fact some of them were considered slaves. There is no doubt in D'iakonov's opinion that the typical exploited person in ancient times generally (and by implication including both the Mediterranean Basin during classical antiquity and the ancient Near East, and even China and India, although these countries are not mentioned here) was the slave, just as the typical exploited person in medieval times was the serf. *The transformation of the slave into the actual property of the slaveowner was merely a special case of the application of noneconomic compulsion to a person deprived of the means of production.*

It seems to me possible to unify all these people under the designation of *ancient unfree people of slave type*. They made up one of the two antagonistic classes of ancient society – a class deprived of ownership of means of production and exploited by a non-economic method; one of its groups – sometimes more numerous, sometimes less – was made up of slaves in the proper sense.[68]

Finally, D'iakonov has this to say about the status of ordinary commune-members – and his statement is extremely significant for the interpretation of the earlier debate on the Asiatic mode of production and its outcome:

From my point of view, the communal citizenry (peasantry) *as such* – as a definite social group, as distinct from certain luckless representatives of it – was not in principle subject to exploitation; it, and only it, possessed full civil rights; even the richest and most distinguished people, including royal functionaries, in order to possess these rights, had to be – or become – commune members. In my opinion, the formula as to the exploitation in ancient Europe of slaves, and in the ancient East, as distinct from Europe, allegedly of 'slaves and the communal peasantry,' is a mere compromise between the points of view of the supporters of slaveholding in the ancient East – primarily V.V. Struve – and the adherents of feudalism in the ancient East during the discussion on social orders in the 1930s. This formula signifies the recognition of a basic and primeval difference in relationships of production between Europe and the East; it is unacceptable both on theoretical grounds and because of non-correspondence with the data of the sources. However different the position of the free peasant in Greece and Babylonia may have been in terms of the political structure of society, they did not differ essentially in respect of socio-economic positions. Both groups had certain obligations to the community and to the state. Both groups possessed the maximum of civil capacity for the given society and both groups were organized into various commune structures, which constituted forms of organization not of *dependent* people (as under feudalism), but precisely of those with the most complete rights.[69]

The following theoretical questions and difficulties come to mind when we consider the line of argument just set forth. I should emphasize here that I'm speaking merely in terms of common sense and Marxist methodology, without in the least calling into question either the data cited by D'iakonov or his specialized interpretation of them.

(1) The distinction between ownership and tenure or possession introduced in the quotation cited on p. 89 may be valid enough in terms of the law of that time and of the data in the sources, but it looks a trifle scholastic in the context. It would seem that when someone, by virtue of holding a particular office or performing a specified service, has access to means of production and has the right to be the tenant or possessor of certain lands (regardless of formal ownership), then to that extent we have before us a manifestation of the Asiatic mode of production as defined, not indeed by Marx – who after all did not have access to these data – but by the 'classical' Aziatchiki of the 1920s; or, to put it another way, we are looking at a member of a corporately organized ruling class coterminous with the state itself. This system also bears a certain formal and outward resemblance to the social order characteristic of medieval European feudalism, but in that case, the services on which tenure of land nominally 'in the king's gift' was predicated, had either a purely military character or a largely fictive one, and the real power under ordinary conditions rested with the feudal lord who also had the right to a preemptive share of the surplus product. In the societies with which D'iakonov is dealing, on the other hand, these services which conferred rights to tenure of the means of production were quite real and of very definite economic value.

(2) With regard to the presence or absence of private ownership of the means of production in the ancient East, and also to the status of 'free' commune-members: granting that there was private ownership in some form and degree, and granting also that taxation is *not necessarily* equivalent to exploitation ('even Rockefeller pays taxes'), the proper question to ask is not, 'Who holds formal titles to the means of production?' but rather, 'What actual

advantages accrue to the owner as contrasted with the nonowner?' After all, a situation is theoretically possible in which, while the means of production are formally in the hands of private individuals or nonstate corporations, the state takes all (or the lion's share) of the surplus product in the form of taxes and other dues, and in addition can draft the local population for compulsory work on state projects. If such a situation existed, the social order so constituted would in fact differ significantly both from that characteristic of Greco-Roman antiquity and from the ordinary kind of feudalism. *Whether* such a situation existed at any particular place and time is of course an issue of fact and of interpretation of the sources. Getting the right answers depends, in this case as in others, on asking the right questions.

(3) Finally, in regard to points made in the last quotation: the equation between the status of the 'free peasantry' in the ancient Near East and in the world of classical antiquity appears to rest on some highly questionable assumptions. First of all, the possession of full civil rights is by no means incompatible *in principle* with *economically* exploited status, although there is a tendency, particularly at earlier historical stages, for civil rights to be limited or lost when such exploitation has been in force for some time. Second, I believe that D'iakonov is assuming that the material obligations of both groups to the state or to the community are similar. The point here is that, to the best of my knowledge, the Greek city-states and the early Roman Republic did not, in principle and under ordinary circumstances, tax their own citizens. The contributions levied during national emergencies, which in principle had to be approved by the citizenry in open meetings, are another matter, and so are the so-called 'liturgies' or compulsory services to the state (equipping and staffing of warships or military units, financing of festivals, public games, and dramatic performances) which were imposed on citizens

with a certain amount of wealth. Neither of these types of measures can be legitimately equated with regular taxation – still less with the partial or total confiscation of the surplus product, the proceeds of which go to support a permanent bureaucracy. D'iakonov has a legitimate point when he attacks the contention (now somewhat antiquated, and by no means shared by all Soviet scholars)[70] that whereas only slaves were exploited in classical Europe, slaves and the communal peasantry jointly were the object of exploitation in the ancient Near East. But of the two possible ways to counter this contention, D'iakonov has, in my opinion, chosen the less valid one: he might better have stated that, in ancient Europe as well, the free peasantry (which, incidentally, was not always communal in the same sense as in the Near East), was exploited to a considerable degree.

D'iakonov continues his analysis of the ancient Near Eastern social order in a second extended article with a somewhat different emphasis (see note 63). Since this work is available in a more than adequate English translation, and since the issues raised in it are in part highly technical, I will not quote or analyze it in as much detail as the one just discussed. In particular, this second article dealing with the structure and characteristics of the exploited group in the ancient Near Eastern kingdom, lacks the comparative dimension which is the source of the difficulties just set forth. D'iakonov is here engaged in a polemic – a restrained one, and by no means ideological in tone, although he does insist, where necessary, on the basic methodological issues dividing the participants – with two Western scholars (I.J. Gelb and J. Renger) who might be considered Aziatchiki, except that they do not appear to be operating within Marxist 'ground-rules.' D'iakonov shows that the differences between the two types of exploited workers in the ancient Near East, whom Gelb calls 'slaves' and 'serfs,' while they exist, are not significant, at least from the standpoint of Marxist methodology, and that, consequently, 'helots and slaves were merely two strata of one of the same economic class. In the final analysis the differences between them are determined by the existence of two economic sectors within the single mode of production of antiquity.'[71]

The issue here is narrower than in the article previously analyzed, in that D'iakonov confines himself to a discussion of the characteristics of groups of workers who by general consent are exploited, and says nothing about the status of the allegedly free peasantry. Within these restrictions, his argument, as far as I can see, is at least worthy of serious consideration.

In view of the general ignorance and neglect of Soviet research in ancient history on the part of Western scholars, and of its one-sided and malicious treatment at the hands of many of those who do pay attention to it,[72] some recent remarks by M.I. Finley take on added significance. In the course of a general discussion (both substantive and historiographic) of 'classical slavery,' Sir Moses offers a critique of D'iakonov's contentions in the articles with which we have just been dealing – a critique with which, in its substance and in so far as I understand it, I agree. However, since Sir Moses is not familiar with the Russian-language literature preceding and contemporary with D'iakonov's work, he is unable to place this work in its intellectual context, and his judgment on it is therefore unduly harsh. He portrays D'iakonov as being engaged in 'a desperate rearguard action designed to "save the phenomena" of the Engelsian unilinear scheme,'[73] that slaves and helot-serfs are typologically identical, and as showing inadequate knowledge of Greek and Roman conditions.[74] Finally, he contends that D'iakonov's fundamental distinction has been demolished in advance by Zel'in (for discussion of Zel'in's position, see immediately below) and by Hahn,[75] and by implication that D'iakonov uses the concept of 'social formation' in an unacceptable sense.[76] While I would agree that Zel'in's formulation of this matter is preferable to D'iakonov's in certain respects, I do not think that Zel'in attained (or even aspired to) the degree of definitiveness which Finley attributes to him; about Hahn's position I am not at all sure. In any case, there is no doubt in my mind that D'iakonov has made an intellectual advance in respect to the concept of slavery and that later scholars will be obliged to take account of what he says.

If D'iakonov presents the best-informed and most carefully nuanced recent defence of the slaveholding interpretation of ancient Near Eastern society, and therefore the most effective refutation of the Aziatchik position in its current form (even though, as I have tried to point out, D'iakonov's argumentation is not in all respects unassailable), Melikishvili and K.K. Zel'in offer a counter-critique of the concept of the slaveholding social order – either specifically as applied to the ancient Near East (Melikishvili, see note 64) or in the broader context of the Greco-Roman world and the Marxist theory of history generally (Zel'in).[77]

Zel'in's immediate and ostensible purposes in these studies with which we are concerned here are, first, to bring clarity into the semantically confused concept of 'slave' by stating with some precision what are the actual distinguishing features of the category of people called slaves, and, second, to identify – again with a certain degree of precision – the type of social order characteristic of the ancient Near East, and particularly Ptolemaic Egypt. The picture which emerges from Zel'in's work taken as a whole differs sharply from what is generally considered typical either of the Greek city-states of the Periclean age or of Rome in the period of the late Republic or the Empire, even though in all three cases we are presumably dealing with societies based on slavery. In fact, Zel'in's work, again taken as a whole, represents a rather sharp and cogent attack on the slave-owning interpretation of ancient Eastern society (at least for the area and the rather late period in question). We should not conclude that Zel'in intends to adopt or defend the Aziatchik position. But at the same time such is the ultimate result of his argument, since the identification of the society in question as feudal has generally been thought unsatisfactory by Soviet scholars since the 1920s, with a few notable exceptions.

Zel'in begins with an appeal for specific argument on the topic of slavery, and for the integrity of the data, phrased in rather general terms:

> [It] would be incorrect, after taking a taxonomic category as point of departure, to give special value to, or even select, facts that would seem to substantiate it. For example, we must not imply the concept of 'the slavery of classical antiquity' in this fashion and, having decided that slaveholding was dominant in antiquity, proceed to 'discover' slaves (or people who seem to us to have been slaves) – and the more of them the merrier – without particularly considering what was specific in the socio-economic relationships placed under the category 'slavery,' and without establishing with sufficient persuasiveness whether those relationships played a determining role in production. . . .
>
> In the realm of the science of society, we remain now, in some respects, at the same level in the development of systematics that zoology was at over 2000 years ago, when scientists were operating with broad morphological concepts – birds, fishes, quadrupeds – and did not base themselves upon the totality of significant criteria identified as the result of comparison of experimental data, not to speak of the examination of species of animals with consideration of their phylogenesis, ecology, geographic division and other factors on which the 'new,' contemporary systematics bases itself.[78]

Zel'in's attack on the concept of slavery as a tool for use in a Marxist context is based on two major contentions – one negative, the other positive. First, the economic criteria for slave status, as they have been set forth by Soviet scholars up to the point at which Zel'in is writing, are not adequate. Here I will quote his reasoning at length, since the passage in question is not included in the translated version of his paper.

O.O. Kriuger in his well-known study of grain-farming in Ptolemaic Egypt, and Academician Struve in his article[79] proceed from the assumption that the main features of slavery as distinct from serfdom are the non-possession of the means of production by the worker and the application of non-economic compulsion to him. On this basis the day-laborers in Hellenistic Egypt are reckoned as slaves ('temporary slaves').

Such a definition, however, is also insufficiently exact and does not take in the data in the sources in all their distinctiveness. After all, non-economic compulsion was applied not only to slaves but also to serfs. Therefore, in the definition cited, there remains only one distinguishing feature – the non-possession of the means of production by the worker. Whether this feature (united with non-economic compulsion) is necessary and sufficient to determine whether we are dealing with slavery in this or that particular case will be made clear below. Let us note here only that Struve's argument of a general nature – 'In Ptolemaic Egypt, as in any slaveholding society, slaves and free people were contrasted with each other' – has no probative force for validating the above-cited definition of slavery, since, in the first place, we do not find this a contrast only in the law of a slaveholding society (compare, for example, the barbarian law codes of the early Middle Ages), and in the second place, this contrast concerns, not both of the features indicated in the definition, but only the second: that is, non-economic compulsion. However, non-economic compulsion is a phenomenon so widespread in pre-capitalistic societies that this feature is obviously insufficient for declaring a person a slave; in the third place, in legislative documents and other sources we find a social division not by the economic index (the presence or absence of means of production, the exploitation of the labor of slaves by slaveowners); but by the juridical: people are divided into freemen and slaves. Both are distinguished, when it is a matter of levying fines or punishments, or, on the contrary, of conferring awards. However, in the legal sources we often do not find answers to the questions of who these slaves are, or what they do, etc.[80]

The complete lack of the means of production by the worker, while not diagnostic for slavery in the strict sense, is still involved in it,

> since it is precisely the absence of the means of production which compelled the poor Athenian citizens to hire themselves out for 'slave-like tasks' . . . and these slave-like tasks – i.e. physical labor – threatened the poor with loss of rights: that is to say, with being declared slaves.[81]

So much for the negative argument. On the positive side, Zel'in points out that class relationships of the type characteristic of capitalist society are based on an assumption of equality before the law which is not found at earlier historical stages. Precapitalist societies usually contain both classes distinguished by the relationship of their members to the means of production, and castes – that is, ranked juridical categories of people – which frequently and in large part failed to coincide with the classes. The existence of these castes prevents groups of people similar in their relationship to the means of production from coalescing into unified and conscious classes. The juridical distinctions between people are enforced by the full physical power of the state, which prevents the fundamental Marxist law – according to which the structure of society is ultimately determined by the relationships of production – from operating at full force and without hindrance, as it does under capitalism. Zel'in himself expresses this idea as follows:

> At early stages in social development, the use of force in economic relationships by individuals or the state (and other juridical entities) was unavoidable. Compulsion was a necessary component of the economic system. *Public law in general is no mere element of the superstructure, and in precapitalistic societies it is indissolubly associated with the economy and serves as an expression of that economy*, inasmuch as the latter is based upon extra-economic compulsion. The law states, in general form, to whom compulsion may be applied, and, in part, what kind of compulsion is applicable.[82]

The attentive reader who has some familiarity with the standard Soviet notion of the Marxist method will not fail to realize that Zel'in has here undertaken a revision – modest at first glance, but actually quite far-reaching – of this method, although I would contend that what Zel'in proposes is not revisionist in terms of the ideas of Marx and Engels themselves. In fact, the emphasized portion in the quotation above is reinforced by a quotation from (apparently) *Anti-Dühring*.

Zel'in expresses the intersection of slaves-as-a-caste with slaves-as-a-class by means of a diagram of intersecting shaded circles, and he contends that only those falling into the area common to both circles – that is, those who are both slaves in the juridical sense and also deprived of the

101

means of production and subject to extra-economic compulsion – should be considered true slaves for the purpose of analysis of the society in question. Under this procedure, the applicability of the concept of the 'slaveholding' social order proves to be very much restricted relative to the way it was used by Soviet scholars in the recent past (up to, say, the mid-1960s), and is still used in the standard textbooks and by D'iakonov. In fact, anyone employing Zel'in's methodology would inevitably be led to the conclusion that the 'classical' social order, as defined by Marx and Engels, is an aberrant phenomenon rather than a universal stage of human history, and hence should not be a tool of Marxist analysis. Zel'in does not say this in so many words, but his reasoning is admirably clear and persuasive throughout, and there is no doubt whatever about where he stands.

Zel'in's analysis of the social structure of Ptolemaic Egypt is of considerable interest as an example of the results of practice of his methodological innovation. He portrays the Ptolemies as supervising and benefiting from a command economy of a type which in modern times would be called state capitalist, and a 'bureaucratic–collectivist' governmental system. In this situation, the immediate producers were for the most part not true slaves by Zel'in's earlier, restrictive definition, since they had at least conditional access to means of production. Groups of true slaves were used for certain special purposes such as work in the gold mines of Nubia, but these were slaves of the state, not of private individuals. Whereas in the Greek *poleis* of the classical period (and for that matter in the Roman Republic as well) slaves were one of the three basic categories of residents, along with free citizens and foreigners, in the Hellenistic state, slaves were only one of the categories of dependent persons, and the important factor here was dependence not on a private individual but on the state.

This dependence is manifested not in the fact that the entire population is subject to the Ptolemies and owes the state certain obligations and taxes, but in the fact that compulsion by the state is the major goad which sets the entire economic mechanism into action. . . . If Marx raised objections to those who thought that the economic sphere was determining only for societies of recent times, these objections were entirely correct, inasmuch as the political sphere, in the thinking of his opponents, was counterposed to the economic one and was taken in isolation. We wish to say something entirely different from what was said by the opponents of Marx: even in ancient times the economy had the same significance as in modern times, but one of the elements of this economy was politics.[83]

If Zel'in's work, just considered, illustrates one aspect of the neo-Aziatchik (or anti-slaveholding) argument, then G.A. Melikishvili can be said to approach the same argument from the other end. Essentially, the anti-Aziatchik position in its contemporary form assumes a fundamental identity between the social order of the ancient East and that of the classical Mediterranean world; any position which denies or tends to qualify this identity is to that extent pro-Aziatchik. Melikishvili emphasizes the relatively untrammeled nature of private property and the prevalence of slaveholding by private individuals in the Greco-Roman world, in contrast to the heavy predominance of the state sector in the economies of the ancient Near Eastern kingdoms.[84] Melikishvili's argument is marred, in my opinion, by uncritical adoption of the parallel between Greco-Roman and early capitalist society, which goes back to Rostovtzeff, and which is also used, though more cautiously, by other Soviet classical historians, such as E.M. Shtaerman.[85]

However, the argument does not stand or fall on the

validity or otherwise of this parallel. As is true in many other cases, Melikishvili's argumentation here seems considerably more sound than his positive suggestions or final conclusions. He cogently questions the interpretation of Spartan helotry (and similar institutions in ancient Thessaly and Crete) by D'iakonov and G.F. Il'in, among other Soviet historians, who see it as a form of exploitation typical of the ancient Near East and therefore a link between it and the Greco-Roman world. According to Melikishvili, this is unjustified because helotry and similar phenomena arose as a result of conquest and subjugation of one ethnic group by another: in other words, it is analogous to what existed in the early feudal societies of northwestern Europe after the fall of the Roman Empire, rather than to the situation in Egypt or the Fertile Crescent. Melikishvili may also dispute D'iakonov's sharp distinction between the public and private sectors in the kingdoms of the ancient Near East, contending that this made little practical difference to the people employed in these sectors.[86]

It is on this point that the issue between the proponents and the opponents of the Asiatic mode of production, in its present form, emerges most clearly. Was there exploitation of the rank-and-file commune-members as such in the kingdoms of the ancient East? If there was, then the social order which prevailed there can by no means be equated with that characteristic of the Greco-Roman world, where it is generally conceded that no such exploitation took place (except in atypical cases like that of the Spartan helots, which can be accounted for by special circumstances), and where in fact the commune itself as a landowning body ceased to exist at a very early date. But if the commune-members of the ancient Near East can be shown to have been in general immune from exploitation, then the slaveholding interpretation of ancient Eastern society – or perhaps it would be better to say, the concept of the single social order of ancient times, however we designate it – is still viable.

It is curious that although Melikishvili argues throughout this article for a consistently neo-Aziatchik position, he comes out at its conclusion in favor of a definition of the social order of the ancient Near East as prefeudal or proto-feudal. Quite apart from its weaknesses in terms of Marxist theory, this usage is likely to involve some difficulties, since it conflicts with that adopted by Soviet historians of early medieval Europe, such as A.I. Neusykhin,[87] who used the same term to designate the social order of the barbarian states of early medieval Europe – that is to say, an early or undeveloped form of feudalism as the term is conventionally used.

It is quite clear that in ancient Egypt, in the Fertile Crescent, or in pre-Hellenistic Asia Minor we are dealing with an entirely different state of affairs, despite certain formal similarities. This conclusion of Melikishvili's looks like evidence of vacillation on his part, and certainly does represent a weakness in his work, but its importance to the central theme of the present monograph should not be overestimated. It is improbable that any Soviet scholar of the 1970s would write in terms of the Asiatic mode of production (except when discussing the history of the field), if only because the geographical form of the concept would seem out of date and out of place in the current context. However, if the material reviewed in the last few pages shows anything, it proves that the debate on the social order of the ancient Near Eastern kingdoms, and as to whether this social order (whatever it may have been) can essentially be equated with that of Greco-Roman antiquity, has continued in full force until extremely recent times. If there has been any attempt to settle these questions *ex cathedra*, I have not seen it. If there has been disciplinary action against any of the participants on either side *in this particular debate*, there is no evidence of it in the public record to my knowledge.[88]

It is more than a little curious that as late as 1972, the well-known and highly popular general circulation journal, *Novyi mir*, published a lengthy essay in which the theory of the Asiatic mode of production was set forth in almost pure form without the term itself being mentioned. The significance of this publication lies in the fact that it presents a very definite point of view on the debate which has been considered in part two to an audience of 'lay intellectuals' – the educated but nonspecialized Soviet reader. The point of view presented here is precisely the one which was increasingly criticized and rejected by scholars and by those who undertook the task of setting the ideological direction of Soviet scholarship beginning approximately in the early 1970s, and whose writings have been reviewed in the last few pages.

The authors define the state in the ancient East (particularly China) in terms which will be familiar to anyone who has studied the works of the classical Aziatchiki of the 1920s, such as, for example, the textbook of political economy by Bogdanov and Stepanov.

> The state in the Eastern countries, as everywhere in the world, was a product of the irreconcilability of class interests; it arose in an atmosphere of fierce social conflicts and was accompanied by the enslavement of certain social forces by others. But in this portion of the human ecumene, as Engels repeatedly emphasized, 'political dominance was everywhere based on the performance of some socially imperative function,' and it 'proved long-lasting only when it performed that socially imperative function.' The ruling strata and groups seized control primarily of the economic, political, and military functions of the state, and usurped primarily *not the means of production as such but their management; they appropriated not the*

primary conditions of labor but their results. They tried, not without success, to clothe their egoistic interests in the impersonal form of a common goal, seeking to give their actions the *appearance* of the pure and independent will of the state.[89]

In this passage, Ostrovitianov and Sterbalova come very close to a position which was considered a deviation from orthodox Marxism during the first debate – namely, that under the Asiatic mode of production, the ruling class achieved its dominant position by performing socially useful functions, and by acquiring effective control over the means of production, but not actual ownership. On the first point the authors speak, not of socially useful functions as such, but of the *official* functions of the state (economic, political and military) – which would imply that the ruling class itself was identical to and coextensive with the state apparatus; this was one of the hallmarks of the Asiatic mode of production in the classical view.

The authors now proceed to an analysis of the society of Imperial China – not as a particular and isolated case, but as the finished and crystallized form of a particular kind of social order. This social order is the product of two intersecting lines of class formation, vertical and horizontal.

The administrative machinery of state power produced out of itself, *vertically*, the higher, middle, and lower groups of the bureaucracy, whose social positions depended entirely on the official posts they held in government service. The authorities, official posts, formal rank, and increased personal wealth resulting from them *did not become hereditary privileges firmly attached to some particular economically dominant class*.[90]

In the horizontal dimension, each rural community in ancient China reproduced within itself a complete set of administrative functions. This apparatus included elected councils of elders, village headmen, people responsible for the groups of five or ten households into which each village was divided, and heads of police detachments. This structure was supervised and administered by the Shen-shih – that is, those members of the literate, bureaucratic class who do not happen to hold an office in the bureaucracy at the particular time in question. This group was highly differentiated within itself, some members of it being 'on the way out' while the advancement of others had been blocked and still others merged with the peasant masses, appearing as wandering astrologers, poets, monks and mystics of various kinds, who in certain ways articulated the views and desires of the people *vis-à-vis* the regime.

Various opinions, of course, are possible as to the validity of this analysis of ancient Chinese society. For instance, one may wonder whether the bureaucratic élite was really a non-self-perpetuating group unconnected with a particular economically dominant class, and whether the facts might not be better interpreted in the sense that the examination system was merely a secondary feature of the class structure – a means of direct investment in social mobility, similar to the mechanism by which the sons of prosperous yeomen, artisans, and merchants in seventeenth- and eighteenth-century England and France could move into the category of 'gentry' through the purchase of military commissions or the acquisition of legal or theological training. Our concern here, however, is not with the merits of the case but with the fact that the educated but unspecialized Soviet reader is being invited to consider a social order which does not fit the standard Marxist definition either of feudalism or of slaveholding, and which therefore throws into question the traditional five-step model. Ostrovitianov and Sterbalova have in essence described the kind of 'bureaucratic collectivism' which was characteristic of the society marked by the Asiatic mode of production as understood by the Aziatchiki of the 1920s – whether orthodox Marxists or dissident, such as Wittfogel. Although the political scientist Richard Kosolapov, who supplies an afterword to this article, is at some pains to distinguish between the authors' views and those of current 'revisionists' such as Roger Garaudy, and to emphasize the potential of flexibility within the traditional five-step model, the implication remains clear that there are aberrant cases which have to be accounted for, and, even if the concept of the Asiatic mode of production is ultimately rejected, this is not the end, but only the beginning of the intellectual process.

Before completing our substantive investigation and going on to our conclusions, we must deal with what is to date the most significant Soviet attempt to summarize the discussion on the Asiatic mode of production and draw conclusions from it – Iu. V. Kachanovskii's *Slaveholding, Feudalism, or the Asiatic Mode of Production?*[91] This book is not and cannot be definitive, for three quite simple reasons. First of all, its appearance predates the most recent work of D'iakonov and Melikishvili, with which we have just dealt, as well as that of other participants in the discussion, such as Shtaerman. Second, Kachanovskii makes no claim to impartiality, but takes an explicitly anti-Aziatchik position, presenting himself as the defender of what he regards as Marxist orthodoxy – although, like most participants in the current debate, he forgoes political invective. Third, Kachanovskii shows little familiarity with the detailed historical and paleographic work done by Soviet scholars on the states of the ancient Near East – work on which the recent version of the Aziatchik position is largely based. It is of course difficult to say whether this silence on Kachanovskii's part is the result of actual ignorance or represents a tactical device.

In the opening pages of his book, Kachanovskii sets forth with admirable clarity the actual state of the question as to the Asiatic mode of production at the present time, and the line-up forces ranged in support of and against this concept. The Asiatic mode of production is defined (by those who assume its existence) in three distinct ways: first as an obligatory transitional stage between preclass (or classless) and class society, through which all of the people of the East and West have passed;[92] second, as a stage which existed only in those countries where natural conditions require large-scale irrigation (a viewpoint most prominently represented by E.S. Varga); and, third, as a mode of production marked by a form of exploitation based on debt-bondage (a view identified with Iu. I. Semenov and Iu. M. Garushiants).[93]

In accordance with these three alternative views on the Asiatic mode of production, Kachanovskii formulates four fundamental questions which his book is intended to answer, as follows:

> Did there exist one more mode of production – the Asiatic – different in principle from slaveholding and feudalism, and accordingly, did there exist one more socio-economic order, the Asiatic? If so, then what is this mode of production [i.e. what are its characteristics]? . . .
>
> Did there exist a transitional state between classless and class societies, which as such had the quality of a special and self-sufficient mode of production (the Asiatic)? . . .
>
> If there was no Asiatic mode of production, then what were the ancient societies – slaveholding or feudal? . . .
>
> Europe, Asia, Africa, and America – are these different paths of historical development or one? Do there exist laws of history, common to all continents? Or must we follow Godelier in recognizing that non-European history follows a different necessity – that is, different laws than the history of Europe?[94]

110

It is worth noting – although Kachanovskii himself does not make this point – that the second and third questions are logically subordinate to the first, in the sense that the second becomes irrelevant if the first is answered negatively, and the third becomes irrelevant if the first is answered positively. However, the fourth question is on the same logical level as the first, and it is described by Kachanovskii as basic and crucial. I would agree, and I would add that this question is what raises the issue of the Asiatic mode of production above the level of a specialized scholarly dispute, and justifies concern with it on the part even of those who are not working within the Marxist tradition.

A large part of Kachanovskii's text is concerned with broad philosophical and methodological issues of the Marxist theory of history, and deals with questions not directly relevant to the Asiatic mode of production. In accordance with the limits placed on our investigation, they are omitted from detailed consideration here. It can, however, be remarked in a general way that Kachanovskii understands the traditional five-step sequence of social orders as a piece of *relative truth* – that is, not absolute, or inviolable, or final – which can be superseded or added to, and does not have to be accepted as an article of faith or rejected as radically wrong, as some scholars are inclined to do. I do not see how, as a general principle, this could be quarrelled with by any well-informed social scientists; but, as we shall see, the implications of this principle as Kachanovskii applies it are something else again.

In his third chapter, 'The Problem of the Pre-capitalist Social Orders and the Conceptual Apparatus of Scholarship,' Kachanovskii has a subsection forthrightly headed 'Can We Scrap the So-Called Five-Step Model?' in which he undertakes a more specific evaluation and defence of this model, precisely as a hypothesis which may or may not adequately account for the known facts. The reader must

111

bear in mind that any defence of the five-part model implies an anti-Aziatchik position, because the traditional list of social orders does not include the one based on the Asiatic mode of production; but, on the other hand, rejection of the five-part model does not in itself confirm the existence of the Asiatic mode of production, because in terms of the Marxist method there are specific criteria which a type of society must meet in order to obtain the status of an independent mode of production or social order.

Kachanovskii sets up two specific conditions which, if they could be found to exist, would imply that the five-step model would be inapplicable outside Europe: first, if in the non-European countries a social order were found which had different characteristics than those which exist in Europe; and, second, if in the non-European countries there were found a reversal of an expected sequence, such as feudalism following capitalism, or slaveholding following feudalism. It is his opinion that no case of either type has been found so far.[95] This implies that the analysis of ancient Chinese society given by Ostrovitianov and Sterbalova (see pp. 106/9, above) is incorrect, or at least that the facts which they cite are open to some other interpretation; likewise, it implies that my objections (see pp. 93–5, above) to D'iakonov's defence of the slaveholding interpretation of ancient Mesopotamian society must somehow be met.

In the last part of the book, Kachanovskii critically analyzes the standard Aziatchik position and finds it deficient because the Asiatic mode of production lacks several of the elements which are needed for a complete and independent social order – for example, a distinctive form of property, which is to say, a distinctive form of relationship between people and the means of production. The most interesting aspect of this argument is a rather subtle polemic with the Hungarian Orientalist Ferenc Tökei, who maintains on the basis of his reading of certain passages in Marx's *Pre-capitalist Economic Formations* that, in societies based on the Asiatic mode of production, exploitation and class antagonism had arisen on the basis of tribal and communal property. It is significant, however, that Tokei's position, to my knowledge, is not shared by any Soviet scholar – and indeed it seems paradoxical from any genuine Marxist point of view. In general, most of the scholars with whom Kachanovskii polemicizes in the second and more sharply focused part of his book are French, or, in a few cases, East German, and therefore much of what he says falls outside the area with which this monograph deals. However, Kachanovskii's critique of the interpretation of the Chinese Shen-shih as a class in the strict Marxist sense is of some interest and deserves quotation *in extenso*, since it speaks directly to the issue which was addressed to Ostrovitianov and Sterbalova in their popular essay, analyzed a few pages earlier.

What was the basis of the appropriation of the surplus by the ruling class [i.e., in this case, the Shen-shih]? In particular, from what sources did the money come which was paid to the Shen-shih who was in the service of the state? The door to higher position and to the acquisition of wealth with which land could be bought was open to the person who had successfully passed through the competitive examination on Confucian literature. If this was the case, then is it a correct conclusion that the basis of property and land was the knowledge of Confucian wisdom? We think not. *The examinations provided the possibility of penetrating into the ruling class, and of taking advantage of those sources of income which were already at its disposal, and which were based on ownership of land (by the state and by private feudal lords) existing even before a particular Shen-shih passed through the examination process.*[96]

This passage, incidentally, brings out an important point, not, in my opinion, sufficiently emphasized by Marxist theorists – namely the need to distinguish between the nature and role of a class as such and the means of recruitment to it (compare the italicized part of the quotation on p. 113). The methodological point made here seems sound, but it is worth noting that it does not foreclose entirely the possibility that we may be dealing in the Chinese case with a social order distinct from those of the Greco-Roman world and of feudal Western Europe (or feudal Russia), since the author admits the possibility of state ownership of the bulk of the land as the basis of an exploitative social order, with appropriation of the surplus product by the ruling class. In the following passage, Kachanovskii deals directly with this problem, in combating the theory of Asiatic class structure put forward by Jean Chesneaux, who contends that under the Asiatic social order the members of the rural communes were exploited by the state as such. Kachanovskii writes:

Can the state as such, and on the other hand the rural communes as such, constitute classes?

If the state possesses ownership of the means of production, plays a particular role in the social organization of labor, appropriates a portion of the wealth, exploits the working people, then does not it become in this case a class in itself? After all, many states of the East externally seem to possess the traits of a class: they were the owners of land and irrigation facilities, they played an important role in the organization of irrigation, agriculture, crafts, construction; they appropriated a significant part of the national income; they exploited the peasants. But the state in and of itself never was a class and never could be. A class is a group of people occupying a particular economic position. The traits of a class characterize the place of this group in the system of social production. As for the state, it is also a group of people, but with other traits – organized and armed, united in an apparatus for the support of political power. An organized and armed group (the state) serves the interests of the economically dominant class.

Let us admit now that both groups coincided – that the ruling class was completely merged with the personnel of the state apparatus. May we in such a case say that 'the state itself as a unit . . . actually receives benefit from the exploitation'? We think not. The 'actual benefit of the state itself' which allegedly exists apart from the benefit to particular physical persons, is an illusion. Behind the benefit to the state or even to an individual organ of it, there always stand in the final analysis the interests of certain concrete living persons. The ruling class may be the personnel of the state apparatus (if it occupies a particular position in the economy), but not the state as such – as a kind of being which does not depend on any group of people. The state in general never exists outside and apart from human groups. . . .

If we encounter a state which possesses ownership of the means of production, appropriates a part of the national income, and plays some role in the economy, this means that the particular state, in the interests of its masters, exercises not only political but also economic functions. Ownership by the state and its exploitation of the peasant commune members – all this is exercised in the interests of those people who hold in their hands the power and direct the work of the state apparatus.[97]

Pursuing this line of reasoning, Kachanovskii next gives a brief but hard-hitting critique of the theory of Bonapartism, according to which the state can, under certain conditions, operate independently of the interests of any particular class. Even in this case, the advantage that the state pursues is not its own mythical advantage, but the very narrow class advantage of the upper bureaucracy. While admitting the possibility of the situation described by Chesneaux, Kachanovskii rejects the conclusions which Chesneaux draws.

> Chesneaux is right in asserting that the tenure of land was frequently given in *precarium* – that is, could be taken away at any moment. He is also right in the sense that the exploiters (the bureaucracy, the aristocracy) appropriated the surplus labor of the commune-members by the authority of the superior state organs. But can we draw from this the conclusion that in the Eastern despotisms, the master and the ruling class was not a group of people (the bureaucracy and aristocracy), but the state itself as such, which these people served, and to which they subjected themselves, and from which they received authority for exploitation. We reply to this question in the negative. No: the master was still the group of people, and the state was a tool in its hands.[98]

Even in a case where there was no private property whatever, and where all the land was held in *precarium* by members of the bureaucracy, the entire bureaucracy could not be dismissed and expropriated at once, although any individual bureaucrat was subject to such measures.

This part of Kachanovskii's argument, although sound enough in formal Marxist terms, begs the question of how the social order which Chesneaux describes (and the possibility of whose existence Kachanovskii admits) is to be classified. Certainly, it does not seem to bear much resemblance to the slaveholding social order, as this is customarily spoken of by Marxist scholars. What Chesneaux describes is generically similar to feudalism, in that it appears to be based on partial or conditional access by the immediate producer to the means of production, modified by noneconomic compulsion. In this sense, Kachanovskii would seem to be advocating a return to the intellectual status quo as of approximately late 1932 – before Struve publicly abandoned the feudal interpretation of ancient Eastern society, and was eventually followed in this by virtually the entire Soviet 'ancient-historical' establishment. The difficulty here, of course, is that if the slaveholding social order is retained at all, we get a reversal of sequence in certain highly significant areas, with slaveholding society following upon feudal society in Ptolemaic (as contrasted to Pharaonic) Egypt, Hellenistic Asia Minor, and classical Greece (as contrasted with Minoan civilization).

Before closing the discussion of Kachanovskii's work and venturing a final over-all judgment on it, we must consider his treatment of the slaveholding formation as such, which presents a number of curious and interesting features. Kachanovskii's chapter 12, 'On the Concepts of "Slaveholding" and "Feudalism",' reproduces the text of an earlier article,[99] with some significant additions. In this chapter, the author presents an analysis of 'classical' slaveholding society, which echoes generally the points made by S.I. Kovalev in his 1933 paper – but without referring to this text. In particular, Kachanovskii specifies that Greco-Roman society cannot be considered a model of the slaveholding order, if only because it included, along with slaves and slave-owners, a large category of formally independent peasants who were exploited chiefly by means of usury. Kachanovskii distinguishes between slaveholding and feudalism by asserting that the latter is based on: (1) a higher level of development of the forces of production, which brings it about that only the surplus product is appropriated, this being sufficient to maintain the ruling class; (2) petty peasant farming and craft production as the foundation of the economy; and (3) limitation of the

monopolistic property of the ruling class to land,[100] with the
dependent population paying rent (in money, in kind, or in
labour) but remaining in possession of the means of production – farms, tools, livestock, etc.

The following comments on Kachanovskii's attempted
distinction seems to me to be in order. First, with regard to
the expropriation of part of the necessary product by the
ruling class under slaveholding, one would need, in order
to validate this point, to show a higher death-rate among
slaves in the Greco-Roman world than among feudal peasants of the Middle Ages – which would present rather
formidable difficulties. Second, the classical writers on
agriculture put forward a number of ideas on how slaves
should be handled, only some of which fit Kachanovskii's
model, and Greco-Roman literature also contains a variety
of indirect economic data, only some of which, again, is
in agreement with what Kachanovskii says.

At the end of his book, Kachanovskii tackles head-on
the problem of defining the social order to which the
ancient Eastern societies belonged. The results of this
attempt are potentially of great importance, and deserve to
be quoted at some length:

> In deciding the question: to what social order did the
> ancient societies belong) – difficulties arise on account
> of the fact that there existed a very great variety of
> forms of exploitation (slavery of 'classical' type,
> exploitation of various categories of bonded people,
> exploitation of peasant commune-members). The first,
> and a very important, step in the analysis of the
> economic nature of ancient forms of exploitation was
> made, it seems to us, by D'iakonov, who singled out a
> typological category of 'bonded workers of slave type.'
> This category included all those forms in which the
> producer is deprived of ownership of the means of
> production and is compelled to work by direct force.[101]

118

Beyond the limits of the category singled out by D'iakonov (which we will call the 'first' or 'slave' category) there remain the numerous producers of ancient times, who held ownership of the means of production (through the mediation of the communes or by individual families). What was their position? Were they an exploited class?. . .[102]

First, let us attempt to separate out a 'second' typological category and mark its boundaries. It includes the owning producer of ancient times – that is, people who themselves perform work and at the same time are owners of the means of production. This category is extremely broad. It includes all possible varieties of ancient Eastern communal peasants enjoying ownership of the means of production, and also Greco-Roman peasants, and not only the citizens of the *poleis* of early Greece but also the citizens of mature Greco-Roman society (Athens and Rome). How is this 'second' category to be considered? As a working hypothesis, we find it possible to put forward the following considerations.

In the first place, we must guide ourselves by the fundamental peculiarities common to this entire category (the gaining of livelihood by one's own labor, and at the same time ownership of the means of production).

In the second place, we must take into account the multiplicity, sometimes very great, of differences between the concrete varieties entering into this category. One of the main differences apparently consists in the fact that the peasants of the ancient East were members of communal structures and held land through the mediation of the commune. On the other hand, the peasants of the mature Greco-Roman world were citizens of a state, who had basically freed themselves from communal forms; they held land on the basis of private property, by individual families.

In the third place, both the fundamental common ground of the category and the great differences within it become entirely clear and explicable if we take into account its origin: it was a gigantic and more or less deformed fragment of the primitive–communal social order within the framework of the slaveholding formation, just as the class of peasants of modern and contemporary times is a deformed fragment of feudalism within the framework of the capitalist order.[103]

The ancient peasantry, whether in the Near East or in the Greco-Roman world, was deformed under the influence of: (a) pauperization and transformation into an urban proletariat, as in late Republican Rome; (b) internal differentiation of the commune; (c) conquest by slaveholding states and exploitation of the conquered population; and (d) direct exploitation by the ruling class through tax-rental.

In my opinion, the final verdict on Kachanovskii's work must be that it is sound in a critical sense and in terms of formal Marxism, but fails ultimately to be quite convincing on the positive side because of the lack of detailed supporting data and demonstrated familiarity with the empirical material. However, at the end of the passage quoted above, Kachanovskii provides a thought which, as we will see in a moment, can become the kernel of a new theory and suggest a way out of the existing dilemma.

Epilogue: 1975–

In 1975, the second phase of the discussion on the Asiatic mode of production essentially closed. No records of oral discussions or theoretical articles on the topic or specialized factual articles relevant to it (such as D'iakonov's) have appeared, to my knowledge, since this time. On the other hand, I have not seen evidence of either an *ex cathedra* pronouncement on anyone's part to the effect that the discussion is now closed and its results are thus-and-such, or a recantation on the part of those who took the 'losing side.' It seems that the problem has been not so much resolved as temporarily shelved.

The only scholar of any prominence who continued to occupy a straight neo-Aziatchik position – that is, to maintain that there was a radical difference between the social orders characteristic of the ancient Near East and China and of the Greco-Roman world – at the end of the discussion was G.A. Melikishvili. He has published nothing on the topic since that time, and the questions which he raised in argument with D'iakonov have remained unanswered.

A small collection of articles on historical theory, published in 1975, contains a brief and rather perfunctory discussion of slavery by M.A. Korostovtsev.[104] This represents a marked retreat from the point which had been reached at the end of the discussion on precapitalist social orders, since it does not cite any of the discussion materials, and is largely limited to an analysis of the position of Marx and Engels on classical slavery. Considering the volume of material produced during the course of the discussion and the effort expended on it, it seems strange that there should have been no attempt at synthesis other than the Kachanovskii volume, which is actually a piece of special pleading, though in many respects an able and effective one. I, for one, am impelled to the conclusion that the sequence of precapitalist social orders remains on the agenda, awaiting new evidence or new ideas, and that what we are now seeing is a natural pause, with no resolution.

Conclusions

These conclusions will be divided into two parts – the first historiographic, dealing with the character of the debate on the Asiatic mode of production and related phenomena, and the second substantive, containing my assessment of the Marxist theory of precapitalist social orders at this point in its development and my suggestions for overcoming certain difficulties in it. I should emphasize that the second category of the conclusions is purely hypothetical and represents, ideally, the starting-point for a new study rather than the end of one.

At various points in the main text I have called attention to the severe difficulties standing in the way of any simple or linear political interpretation of the debate, even in its early stage, when political invectives and innuendoes were a common feature of it. These difficulties intensify after the revival of the debate in the early 1960s. I have seen no clear evidence of political interference in the form of attempted authoritative statements by political bodies such as the Central Committee, CPSU, or even editorials in the scholarly press. The 'Aziatchik' position – which is to say, the one which denies the identity between the social order typical of the ancient Oriental states and that of classical antiquity – was fully expressed and defended in the renewed debate by scholars such as Melikishvili, though not under that name. Furthermore, it is widely recognized that Marx, at least at one point in his career, held an Aziatchik position. The strictures with regard to the slaveholding social order which were urged by Kovalev in the mid-1930s are generally accepted. The simplest overall conclusion would therefore be that the Aziatchik side, in its new guise, had won the debate in all respects except that of terminology.

Turning to substantive considerations, it seems clear that the social order of classical antiquity is an aberrant case which owes its key position in 'classical' Marxism to the distinctive cultural bias of Marx and Engels, deriving from their position as classically educated intellectuals of the early and middle nineteenth century. All the attempts to equate the 'classical' social order with that of the ancient Near East, Pharaonic Egypt, India or China on any fundamentally simple and straightforward basis seem to me to involve a great deal of artificiality and straining of terms, and some violence to the known historical data – even when these attempts are quite subtle and sophisticated, as in the case of D'iakonov's recent work.

In contrast to the slaveholding social order, both feudalism and capitalism represent clearly delineated systems of relationships – even though capitalism developed only once in world history. At the same time, it should be clear to the reader that I am not an Aziatchik of the classical type. I agree essentially with Nikiforov that any revival of the (or an) Asiatic mode of production at this point must be based on data and considerations of which Marx was not aware – although it should also be based on the principles which informed his thinking. My position can perhaps best be defined as neo-Aziatchik in the sense set forth on page 83. That is to say, I consider it advisable to replace the slaveholding social order with a variable 'prefeudal' stage which can take widely differing forms depending on both natural factors (climate, topography, fertility of the soil, and the like) and particular historical conditions – namely the presence of relatively highly developed cultures and extremely backward ones in close proximity to each other. Furthermore, it would seem that this prefeudal stage is not capable of giving rise to a higher stage out of itself, and that the revolution to which it is subject is a purely destructive one (as many Soviet classical historians, such as Shtaerman, have observed with regard to the slaveholding order). In those cases which follow the 'Asiatic' model, the destructive revolution typically occurs as a result of foreign conquest – not by barbarians, as in the case of the Roman Empire, but by the more highly developed and technologically advanced European societies. What I suggest here looks like a considerable departure from the classical Marxist model, but it should be noted that it does not violate the materialist and evolutionary principle. Society still evolves, but the evolution takes place within progressively larger units, until at the present stage in history, the evolving unit is the world itself.

We have come to the end of our investigation. I hope I have shown that the Marxist theory of history, in its Soviet version, despite the strains placed upon it and the distortion to which it has been subject at various times, remains vital and fruitful and worthy of the attention of scholars holding views which diverge widely from those examined here.

NOTES

Abbreviations

IGAIMK *Izvestiia Gosudarstvennoi akademii istorii material'noi*
      kul'tury
NAA   *Narody Azii i Afriki*
SS   *Soviet Sociology*
SE   *Sovetskaia etnografiia*
SA&A *Soviet Anthropology and Archaeology*
VDI   *Vestnik drevnei istorii*
VI   *Voprosy istorii*

Preface

1 See George Dalton, 'How Exactly are Peasants
"Exploited"?,' *American Anthropologist*, vol. 76 (1974),
pp. 553–61; Stephen P. Dunn, 'On the Exploitation of
Peasants,' *American Anthropologist*, vol. 78 (1976), pp.
639–43, with a reply by Dalton, ibid., pp. 643–5; Peter J.
Newcomer, 'Toward a Scientific Treatment of
"Exploitation": A Critique of Dalton,' *American
Anthropologist*, vol. 79 (1977), p. 115, also with a reply by
Dalton, ibid., p. 125; William Derman and Michael Levin,
'Peasants, Propaganda, Economics, and Exploitation,'
American Anthropologist, vol. 79 (1977) pp. 199ff.

2 See Basile Kerblay, 'Les Enseignements de l'expérience soviétique d'agriculture collectiviste (Resultats, problèmes et perspectives),' *Revue d'études comparatives est-ouest*, vol. 10 (1979), no. 3, p. 7. See also the editorial by Lester Brown, 'Karl Marx was a City Boy,' *Science*, 12 September 1980, p. 1187.

3 'The *virtues* of socialism are not practiced except by a very small number of individuals. For the immense majority of them there exists this fundamental distinction between what belongs to the person himself and requires all his concern and what belongs to the collective – that is, to no-one' (Kerblay, op. cit., p. 27).

4 Barry Hindess and Paul Hirst, *Pre-Capitalist Modes of Production*, London, Routledge & Kegan Paul, 1975.

5 Lawrence Krader, *The Asiatic Mode of Production*, Assen, Netherlands, and New York, Van Gorcum, 1975; Melvin Rader, *Marx's Interpretation of History*, New York, Oxford University Press, 1979.

6 Joseph Schiebel, 'Aziatchina: The Controversy Concerning the Nature of Russian Society and the Organization of the Bolshevik Party,' unpublished doctoral dissertation, University of Washington, 1972.

Part one: Decline and fall

1 For a lucid and useful discussion of major issues in Soviet-Marxist ideology as it relates to social science (on which this paragraph and the following one are largely based), see W.M. Mandel, 'Soviet Marxism and the Social Science,' in A. Simirenko (ed.), *Social Thought in the Soviet Union*, Chicago, Quadrangle Books, 1969, especially pp. 34–5, 39–40.

2 Quoted in Howard Selsam and Harry Martel, *A Reader in Marxist Philosophy*, New York, International Publishers, 1963, p. 187.

3 Mandel, op. cit., pp. 34–5.

4 The Asiatic mode of production, as defined by its proponents, includes a number of elements not mentioned

by Mandel in this passage. These include: (1) the absence of private *ownership* – as distinct from mere possession or tenure for use – of the basic means of production, namely land; (2) the identity between rent and taxes, or, to put it differently, the fact that rents took the form of taxes; and (3) the fact that the ruling class was corporately organized and was coextensive with the administrative apparatus of the state. The question as to whether these and other characteristics of the Asiatic mode of production are to be found in, or are fairly deducible from, the works of Marx, or whether, on the other hand, they have been developed by later Marxist scholars, is a complex one which will have to be left open for the time being. However, for a compilation of quotations from the works of Marx and Engels on this issue, and a preliminary discussion of it, see the two-part article by N.B. Ter-Akopian, 'Razvitie vzgliadov K. Marksa i F. Engel'sa na aziatskii sposob proizvodstva i zemledel'cheskuiu obshchinu,' *NAA* (1965), no. 1, pp. 74–88, and no. 2, pp. 70–85. It should be borne in mind that some of the texts used by Ter-Akopian in this article were not available to the participants in the debate during the period with which we are concerned in the first section of the present volume.

5 Note that I do not say 'as a result of which.' Judgment should be reserved for the present as to whether the abandonment of the concept of the Asiatic mode of production represented a genuine intellectual shift or was purely the result of a political decision. This is especially true since the use of the concept is open to important (and, in my opinion, at least partly valid) objections from the point of view of pure Marxist theory, which have no direct connection with political matters.

6 See for example N.B. Ter-Akopian, op. cit., part 1, pp. 74–5:

> The concept of the Asiatic mode of production was first advanced by Marx and Engels in the 1850s. . . . The societies based on the Asiatic mode of production were defined by Marx and Engels as systems of agricultural communes. The self-sufficient nature of these communes, their isolation from each other, necessarily led to the development of a despotic state, whose functions included control over the forces of nature (the most vivid example

of which is the creation of systems of irrigation) *and the defense of common interests.* . . . It is true that in such works of Lenin as the 'Lecture On The State' we do not find mention of the Asiatic mode of production. But in itself this fact as yet says nothing; after all, in the late works of Marx and Engels we do not encounter the term Asiatic mode of production (which is explained, in particular, by the fact that historical scholarship confirmed the hypothesis of the founders of Marxism as to the universal distribution of the agricultural commune – the basis of the so-called Asiatic mode of production. But we also do not find, either in Marx or in Engels or in Lenin, any hints that the concept of the Asiatic mode of production has been abandoned (emphasis mine).

7   *Diskussiia ob aziatskom sposobe proizvodstva*, Leningrad, GSEI, 1931, p. 22. Hereinafter cited as *DASP*.
8   In the technical Marxist sense of centralized factory production without the use of machines.
9   *DASP*, p. 71.
10 Ibid., p. 72.
11 See K.A. Wittfogel, *Oriental Despotism: A Comparative Study of Total Power*, New Haven, Yale University Press, 1957, pp. 375–8.
12 Ibid., pp. 378–80, 389–94.
13 Since Lenin always insisted that he was not a revisionist – that is, never repudiated any position taken by Marx subsequent to the publication of the *Communist Manifesto*, but merely *added* to the Marxist canon his own interpretation of events and situations which arose after Marx's death – it may be thought that whenever Lenin quoted Marx he was thereby also stating his own position. Wittfogel, however, does not and cannot use this argument, which would require him to recognize Lenin's status as a nonrevisionist Marxist. Furthermore, even if this reasoning is valid, it does not affect the merits of Wittfogel's interpretation which assumes an abrupt change in 1915 in Lenin's views concerning the Asiatic mode of production, made for intellectually dishonest reasons – or those of my argument here, in so far as it is directed against such an assumption.
14 V.I. Lenin, *Sochineniia*, Moscow, Gospolitizdat, 4th edn, 1967, vol. 20, p. 375.

15 Wittfogel, op. cit., p. 379.
16 Ibid., p. 380.
17 V.I. Lenin, op. cit., vol. 6, p. 28.
18 V.I. Lenin, *Collected Works*, Moscow, Progress Publishers, 1965, vol. 10, pp. 331–2. The emphasis in the first part of the quotation is my own.
19 *DASP*, p. 145.
20 L. Mad'iar, foreword M. Kokin and G. Papaian, *Tszin-Tian'. Agrarnyi stroi drevnego Kitaia*, Leningrad, 1930, p. lviii. Unfortunately, neither this volume nor Mad'iar's own book (*Ekonomika sel'skogo khoziaistva v Kitae*, Moscow, Giz, 1928), which sparked this whole discussion, are available to me at this point.
21 *DASP*, p. 168.
22 See V.I. Lenin, *Collected Works*, vol. 29.
23 Karl Marx, *Capital*, New York, International Publishers, 1967, p. 791. I was unable to locate the second part of this quotation in Marx's text.
24 *DASP*, p. 78.
25 Stephen P. Dunn, 'The Position of the Primitive Communal Social Order in the Soviet Marxist Theory of History,' in *Toward a Marxist Anthropology*, New York, Mouton Publishers, 1979, pp. 173–84.
26 *DASP*, pp. 79–80.
27 S.M. Dubrovskii, *K voprosu o sushchnosti 'aziatskogo' sposoba proizvodstva, feodalizma, krepostnichestva i torgovogo kapitala*, Moscow, Izdatel'stvo Nauchnoi assotsiatsii vostokovedeniia pri TsIK SSSR, 1929, p. 17.
28 Marx, *Capital*, vol. 3, p. 804. This formulation, which implies that the slave economy, or the slaveholding social order, is equivalent to any kind or degree of prevalence of slavery, contrasts somewhat oddly with the way slaveholding society is now viewed by most Soviet scholars.
29 Dubrovskii, op. cit., p. 44.
30 Ibid., p. 165:

Thus, our task has by no means been to explain the concrete historical development of the Asiatic peoples. Our task has only been to destroy the erroneous conceptions about special modes of production and special paths of development allegedly characteristic of the Asiatic peoples at all stages of their historical development.

31 The text of the debate on the Dubrovskii pamphlet is published in *Istorik-Marksist* (1930), no. 15, as follows: main paper by Malyshev (in two parts) entitled 'O feodalizme i krepostnichestve,' pp. 43–103; debate on this paper, pp. 104–27; and a much shorter paper by A.V. Efimov, 'Kontseptsiia ekonomicheskikh formatsii u Marksa i Engel'sa i ikh vzgliady o strukture vostochnykh obshchestv,' with the debate on it, pp. 128–51. There is no indication as to whether the second paper and debate followed the first directly in the same locale, but in any case most of the speakers were the same.

32 This point is raised by I. Mints (*Istorik-Marksist* (1930), no. 15, p. 113) and A. Udal'tsov (ibid., p. 118), prominent Soviet historians still active today. There does not seem to be any convenient and adequate English translation for the Soviet term *uklad*, and I have therefore adopted it as a technical term in my own work. The best equivalent is probably 'a socio-economic system'; it refers to a type of economic activity, such as individual peasant farming or small-scale craft production (with the social arrangements accompanying it), which may be at variance with the dominant form that determines the character of the social order in a given society.

33 *Istorik-Marksist* (1930), no. 15, p. 144.

34 Ibid., p. 130.

35 Ibid., p. 144. During Dubrovskii's rebuttal, Zor'kii interrupts from the floor to demand that Dubrovskii give an immediate answer as to what he means by the social order and *uklad* of the transitional period; Dubrovskii counters by alleging a misprint in the stenographic record (pp. 157–8). All this would be the stuff of high comedy, if the consequences had not been in some cases so serious.

36 A.A. Bogdanov and I.I. Stepanov, *Kurs politicheskoi ekonomii*, 4th edn, Moscow and Leningrad, Gosudarstvennoe Izdatel'stvo, 1924. A detailed consideration of the complex issues raised by this curious work would be out of place here, but it is interesting to note that the authors define and describe the Asiatic mode of production, and the type of society which arises on the basis of it, in terms entirely consonant with Wittfogel's conception:

The transition of feudal systems into oriental-despotic ones took place where the conditions of 'external nature' – the environment which surrounded the society – demanded a *stable and close unification* which was not characteristic of the feudal system. We know that the external environment for a social system includes not only the elements of physical nature, with which it has to deal in the course of production, but also the other human societies which are unified with it and with which it collides in struggle. . . . There is no doubt that the prototype of the bureaucratic hierarchy was the feudal hierarchy. But there the authoritarian role of the suzerain was limited by virtue of his interests, and this limitation was validated by customary law. The suzerain has neither the need, nor is it to his advantage, to intervene in the economic activity of his vassals . . . as long as the quitrent and the corvée are correctly paid; and by the same token there is no need of, or advantage in, increasing either [of these] to the detriment of the vassal's welfare, as long as the feudal lord's own economy remains primarily on a subsistence basis, since in this case his requirements cannot rise with any degree of speed. But with the transformation of a part of the feudal state into a bureaucratic despotism, all these relationships begin to change rapidly. In their basic task, the bureaucrats were organizers of the permanent, central state economy – technical, military, and of course, taxational. . . . This economy, extremely large and complex, requires prescriptive discipline, which given authoritarian relationships was possible only through the most complete enslavement of the immediate performers [*ispol'niteli*]. Prisoners of war were used for various state projects, and were the first to become state slaves in the most severe sense; but soon all those from among the subjects of the state proper who have been taken for these projects, are almost or wholly equated with them in this regard. And as the new centralized bureaucratic mechanism develops out of the previous feudal hierarchy, the authoritarian principle is pursued ever more mercilessly in the form of completely unlimited subordination of the lower to the higher, in which the only link in the chain – the despotic monarch who has replaced the supreme suzerain – acquires absolute power over all without exception (pp. 187–9).

This is pure Wittfogelism, even to its elegiac tone and predilection for absolute terms. It is significant that Bogdanov and Stepanov, basing themselves on the Chinese case (rather superficially interpreted, or so at least it seems to me) describe the Asiatic type of despotism as developing out of a feudal system, while Marx, and most other proponents of the Asiatic mode of production during the period with which we are concerned here, place it historically between the primitive–communal and the slaveholding orders. In general the treatment of Eastern society found in this book seems (at least to me) markedly abstract and static, out of tune with the true spirit of Marxism, and indeed in some respects defamatory to the Eastern peoples, with their ancient and rich traditions of civilization: 'About the ideology of such systems there is no need to say much. It is quite clear that it can only be authoritarian through and through in religious forms – stagnant through and through, immobile, hostile to any movement and creativity in any field of social life whatsoever' (p. 192).

37 *Istorik-Marksist* (1930), no. 15, p. 156.
38 *DASP*, p. 80.
39 F. Engels, *Anti-Dühring*, New York, International Publishers, 1939, pp. 197–8:

> As men first emerged from the animal world – in the narrower sense of the term – so they made their entry into history; still half animal, brutal, still helpless in face of the forces of Nature, still ignorant of their own: and consequently as poor as the animals and hardly more productive than these. There prevailed a certain equality in the conditions of existence, and for the heads of families also a kind of equality of social position – at least an absence of social classes – which continued among the natural agricultural communities of the civilised peoples of a later period. In each such community there were from the beginning certain common interests the safeguarding of which had to be handed over to individuals, even though under the control of the community as a whole: such were the adjudication of disputes; repression of encroachments by individuals on the rights of others; control of water-supplies, especially in hot countries; and finally, when conditions were still absolutely primitive,

religious functions. Such offices are found in primitive communities of every period – in the oldest German *Mark* communities and even today in India.

40 Efimov (*Istorik-Marksist* (1930), no. 15, p. 132) appears to consider this at least a possibility: 'Thus, either Marx and Engels consider the Oriental societies slave societies with state ownership of the slaves, or – what is precisely opposite to this – they consider these societies preclass patriarchal societies with a prevalence of clan relationships and clan ownership.'

41 *DASP*, p. 6.

42 Ibid., pp. 59–63.

43 Ibid., p. 53. Kokin's position here is one which many Soviet scholars are currently defending as quite correct Marxism; see L.V. Danilova, 'Controversial Problems in the Theory of Precapitalist Societies,' *SA&A*, vol. 9 (1971), no. 4 (originally published in L.V. Danilova *et al.* (eds), *Problemy istorii dokapitalisticheskikh obshchestv*, Moscow Nauka, 1968; hereinafter referred to as *PIDO*). The current situation will be discussed in more detail below.

44 That is, the apparent coincidence between the Trotskyist position and that of Kokin, Papaian, Varga, Mad'iar, and the Aziatchiki generally.

45 *DASP*, p. 63. The word which I have translated 'prejudice' is *predubezhdenie*, meaning literally 'a conviction before the fact.' In the following sentence, Iolk restates the point even more clearly and forcibly, speaking of 'a biassed [*predvziatoe*] Party attitude.'

46 But in fact no discussion of this point appears in the paper as printed.

47 *DASP*, p. 20.

48 L.V. Danilova, 'Stanovlenie marksistskogo napravleniia v sovetskoi istoriografii epokhi feodalizma,' *Istoricheskie zapiski*, vol. 76, Moscow, Nauka, 1965, p. 99:

The creative initiative of historians was inhibited by the fear of political labels. . . . The denial of feudalism in the East in the precapitalist period and of its very significant survivals in the stage contemporary with the discussion, on the one hand and the evaluation of the national liberation movements (primarily the prospects of the Chinese revolution) on the other, were certainly in direct and immediate dependence. But it would be quite incorrect on this basis to consider every proponent of the Asiatic mode of production a Trotskyist. The wholesale accusations of Trotskyism, which were a direct manifestation of the personality cult, led to some specialists in the history of the ancient and medieval East (for example N. Kokin) being retrained and going over to the study of the recent period. This damaged not only the study of early historical periods but also the development of theoretical questions.

In a later passage (p. 113) Danilova states that various speakers in the course of the 1930 debate (and she cites Zor'kii as an example) attributed to revisionism and to deviations of various kinds certain individual mistakes which were actually due to inadequate command of Marxist theory or of the empirical facts. In other words, these things were mistakes, but not the kind of mistakes they were considered to be at the time. See also Jan Pečirka, 'Von der asiatischen Produktionsweise zu einer marxistischen Analyse der frühen Klassengesellschaften (Randbemerkungen zur gegenwärtigen Diskussion in der UdSSR),' *Eirene*, vol. 6 (1967), pp. 141–75. Special attention should be paid to the relative dates of these works. While Danilova's survey was probably written before the reopening of the discussion on the Asiatic mode of production in the fall of 1964, and one might therefore expect her to show a certain caution in handling this material, Pečirka's paper was written while the discussion was in full swing and appeared in the relatively freer (at least in some respects) atmosphere of Czechoslovakia on the eve of the Prague Spring. It is my impression that had there been authoritative decisions about the concept of the Asiatic mode of production in the printed record, Pečirka would have cited them.

49 Wittfogel, op. cit., pp. 406–8.
50 To the best of my knowledge, no Soviet scholar maintains that Chinese society was slaveholding at any period later than the beginning of the Chou Dynasty. However, see P. Skalnik and T. Pokora, 'Beginning of the Discussion about the Asiatic Mode of Production in the USSR and the People's Republic of China', *Eirene*, vol. 5 (1966), pp. 179–87.

Part two: Resurgence

1 At this point, I must make once more the qualification that I have not yet seen the monographs on ancient China by Mad'iar and by Kokin and Papaian (see part one, note 20) and therefore cannot tell to what extent these works may represent independent and original research.

2 See N.B. Ter-Akopian, 'Razvitie vzgliadov K. Marksa i F. Engel'sa na aziatskii sposob proizvodstva i zemledel' – cheskuiu obshchinu,' *NAA* (1965), no. 1, pp. 74–88, and no. 2, pp. 70–85, and also V.I. Kuzishchin, 'Poniatie obshchestvenno-ekonomicheskoi formatsii i periodizatsiia istorii rabovladel'cheskogo obshchestva,' *VDI* (1974), no. 3, pp. 69–87.

3 See G.A. Melikishvili 'The Character of the Socio-economic Structure in the Ancient East (A Preliminary Classification of Class Societies by Stage and Type),' *SA&A*, vol. 15, (1976–7), nos 2–3, pp. 29–49 (originally published in *NAA* (1972), no. 4); Iu. I. Semenov, 'The Theory of Socioeconomic Systems and the Process of World History,' *SA&A*, vol. 16 (1977), no. 1, pp. 3–26 (originally published in *NAA* (1970) no. 5, pp. 82–95).

4 This paper and the record of the discussion on it were published *IGAIMK*, no. 77: V.V. Struve, 'Problema zarozhdeniia, razvitiia i razlozheniia rabovladel'cheskikh obshchestv drevnego Vostoka,' pp. 32–111; discussion of this paper by other scholars, pp. 112–56; rebuttal by Struve, pp. 157–81. This material is preceded by a relatively brief paper by A.G. Prigozhin, in which he makes some critical observations, and seems to be upholding, in general terms, the feudal interpretation of ancient Eastern society.

5 For detailed information on Struve's career, see D.A. Ol'derogge and V.V. Matveev, 'Vasilii Vasil'evich Struve (1889–1965),' *SA&A*, vol. 7 (1968), no. 2, pp. 52–5. This obituary originally appeared in *SE*.

6 V. Struve, *Diskussia ob aziatskom sposobe proizvodstva*, Moscow and Leningrad, *GSEI*, 1931, pp. 94–5.

7 This typology has been sharply criticized by some Western historians of the ancient economy, such as M.I. Finley: 'We are in thrall to a very primitive sociology which assumes that there are only three kinds of labor status: the free, contractual wage earner, the serf, and the slave.' M.I. Finley, 'The Servile Statuses of Ancient Greece,' *Revue Internationale des droits de L'Antiquité*, series 3, vol. 7 (1960), p. 179. Soviet scholars have also recently attempted to develop a more differentiated model; see K.K. Zel'in, 'The Morphological Classification of Forms of Dependence,' *SS*, vol. 6 (1968), no, 4, pp. 3–24. While detailed examination of this question must await another occasion, it seems to me that a Marxist typology of labor (or more properly, of laboring status) must be based on two intersecting criteria: the laborer's relationship to the means of production, and the character of the compulsion which is applied to him to induce him to work. Each of these criteria has only two possible 'positions': that is to say, the worker either has access to the means of production or lacks it, and he is induced to work either by economic or noneconomic compulsion. The intersection of these criteria can only create a fourfold set of alternatives, and one of these alternatives is inherently unrealizable since access to the means of production rules out the use of economic compulsion as a motivation for labor. Therefore it would seem that a more complex typology of laboring status would presuppose additional criteria not envisaged in any model which is derivable from Marx's thought.

8 This work is cited and summarized in N.M. Postovskaia, *Izuchenie drevnei istorii Blizhnego vostoka (1917–1959 gg.)*, Moscow, Nauka, 1961, pp. 153–4 ff.

9 A.A. Adzhan, *IGAIMK*, no. 77, p. 134.

10 Ibid., p. 151.

11 This phrase is quoted from Struve's remarks at the 1930 discussion on Godes's paper, which I have already described.

12 Struve, *IGAIMK*, no. 77, pp. 171–2.

13 In 1939 Lur'e published a monograph in which he contended that the immediate producers of the category referred to in the ancient Egyptian texts as *mrts* had a right to at least part of the fruits of their labor and thus could not be considered slaves. Accordingly, he continued to argue that the ancient Egyptian social order was an

immature or undeveloped form of feudalism. On this see
N.M. Postovskaia, op. cit., pp. 112 *et seq*.
14 See for example I.M. Lur'e, 'Drevneegipetskie terminy
meret i *khentiushe* vo vremena Drevnego tsarstva' ('The
Ancient Egyptian Terms *Meret* and *Khentiushe* at the
Time of the Old Kingdom'), *VDI* (1951), no. 4, pp. 73–80.
It is interesting that in this very article Lur'e is still
upholding the same factual contentions with regard to the
mrts as he was in 1939, but his interpretation of these facts
has been changed in the light of Struve's research on
Mesopotamia.
15 See particularly N.M. Postovskaia, op. cit., chapters 1–3;
L.V. Danilova, 'Stanovlenie marksistskogo napravleniia v
sovetskoi istoriografii epokhi feodalizma,' in *Istoricheskie
zapiski*, vol. 76, Moscow, Nauka, 1965, pp. 62–119.
Danilova's account, though very valuable, runs only
through the middle 1930s, and the imposition of the
'personality cult' in its most virulent form. She therefore
gives to the process she is describing the aspect of an
intellectual tragedy, and says nothing about the restoration
of more normal conditions later on. Anyone seriously
concerned with the history of Soviet social science before
the Second World War should certainly review the files of
the two periodicals published by Gosudarstvennaia
akademiia istorii materialnoi kultury (GAIMK) – the
quarterly *Problemy istorii dokapitalisticheskikh obshchestv*
(not to be confused with the collection issued under the
same title in 1968) and the monthly *Soobshchenie
GAIMK* – which I do not analyze here, partly for reasons
of space and partly because much of the material in them
falls outside of the area with which I am mainly concerned.
While some of the articles in these journals are marked
(and marred) by the kind of invective which has given
Marxist scholarship a bad name among many people, the
contents as a whole show that it is mistaken to believe that
lively debate on the fundamental issues of the Marxist
method, and on the interpretation of historical fact, ever
died out, even during the darkest days of Stalinism.
16 S.I. Kovalev, 'Ob osnovnykh problemakh
rabovladel'cheskoi formatsii,' *IGAIMK*, no. 64,
Leningrad, 1933. The neglect of this work has been such
that the American Union Catalog specifically lists it as
never having been published. Professor Jan Pečirka of

Prague cites it in one of his German-language surveys of the discussion on the Asiatic mode of production, and it was only through his kindness that I was able to obtain a photostatic copy. I wish to take this opportunity to extend my deepest gratitude to Professor Pečirka for this favour.

17 Ibid., p. 10. Emphasis mine.

18 True, Kovalev tentatively includes Mesopotamia within the circum-Mediterranean area of full-blown slaveholding society, but it is doubtful that he would still have done so had he been writing even in the late 1950s (to say nothing of more recent times) and had access to I.M. D'iakonov's studies and the work of such Western scholars as Thorkild Jakobsen.

19 Kovalev, op. cit., pp. 13–14.

20 V.P. Kobishchanov is an implied exception to this last point, since he advocates an analysis of the social order of classical antiquity which disregards the issue of slavery entirely and proceeds in terms of various forms and gradations of feudalism. Even he, however, leaves open the possibility that a true slaveholding social order – that is, one with the characteristics listed by Marx – may have existed elsewhere or at some other time.

21 V.V. Struve, 'Marksovo opredelenie ranneklassovogo obshchestva,' *SE* (1940), no. 1, pp. 5–27.

22 See Emile Burns (ed.), *A Handbook of Marxism*, New York, International Publishers, 1935, p. 182.

23 K. Marx, *Capital*, vol. 1, New York, International Publishers, 1967, p. 79.

24 V.V. Struve, 'Marksovo opredelenie.'

25 Ibid., pp. 8–10. For the passage by Marx which is at issue here see Marx, *Capital*, vol. I, pp. 333–4.

26 Struve, 'Marksovo opredelenie.'

27 That is, deformed under the influence of a dominant and more advanced social order, as the primitive–communal society of the Witoto Indians was deformed under capitalist influence, in the example mentioned in part one.

28 This idea is developed in greater detail by Iu. B. Kachanovskii, *Rabovladenia, feodalizm ili aziatskii sposob proizvodstva?*, Moscow, Main Editorial Office for Oriental Literature, Nauka Publishing House, 1971, pp. 222–3. This work, and other contributions to the more recent discussion, will be dealt with at greater length below.

29 V.V. Struve, *Istoriia drevnego vostoka*, Moscow, Gospolitizdat, 1941. This second edition, unlike the first, which appeared in 1936 as part of the *History of the Ancient World*, published by GAIMK, contains contributions by other authors on particular areas such as ancient India, the Hittite Empire, and Urartu. This volume remained a standard Soviet textbook on the subject until the early 1950s.

30 Ibid., pp. 67–9. It must be noted that this passage is at variance with both earlier and later statements by Struve and other authors. In his 1934 paper Struve says that the field hands on the royal *latifundia* of the Third Dynasty of Ur worked the year around and therefore could not have had their own farms or means of production; they must have been either slaves or hired hands, but the second possibility is ruled out on other grounds (see *IGAIMK*, no. 77, pp. 54 *et seq.*). It is of course, quite possible that the situation described in the passage quoted above dates from a period earlier than the Third Dynasty of Ur: the passage includes no specific date. Even if we make this assumption, the problem does not disappear, but is merely pushed backward in time; we are still faced with a social order marked by exploitation and extraction of the surplus product from the immediate producers, but which cannot logically be classified as either slaveholding or feudal – in other words, we have before us the set of circumstances identified with the 'Asiatic' social order.

31 There were a few survivors, such as A.I. Tiumenev (1880–1957), but this scholar was unusual in that he had been a trained and committed Marxist since his student days early in the century. For biographical data on Tiumenev see: I.D. Amusin, 'Sotsial' noekonomicheskaia istoriia drevnego mira v trudakh Akademika A.I. Tiumeneva,' in *Problemy sotsial'no-ekonomicheskoi istorii drevnego mira*, Moscow-Leningrad, Izd. AN SSSR, 1963 (a memorial volume for Tiumenev). In addition, some very long-lived scholars remained active into the early 1960s, but these were primarily philologists, trained and working in a somewhat separate tradition with which we are not directly concerned in this paper.

32 The widespread use of slave labor was of course characteristic also of certain forms of early capitalism – most notably the 'plantation economy' of the ante-bellum

American South and the eighteenth- and nineteenth-century West Indies. However, the treatment by Marx of the 'classical' social order in the *Introduction to the Critique of Political Economy*, and of plantation slavery in vol. I of *Capital* makes it quite clear that he considers ancient and modern slavery as two entirely different phenomena. Most modern Marxists have followed his lead in this, although certain ambiguities in the treatment of the topic do occur.

33 I do not know of any full and explicit statement of this position; what I say here is deduced from the Marxist concept of relationships of production and from statements by Marxist thinkers (chiefly Soviet) about the social nature of peasantry.

34 'K izucheniiu istorii krest'ianstva v drevnosti,' *VDI* (1947), no. 1, p. 4. The incorporated quotation is taken from the *German Ideology*; see K. Marx and F. Engels, *Werke*, vol. 3, Berlin, Dietz, 1961, p. 23.

35 This word refers to a primitive or archaic form of slavery, in which, first, slave labor was usually done only for domestic tasks, and not in the production of goods, properly speaking; and, second, there was no sharp juridical distinction between slaves and the other junior members of the household, both categories being equally subject to the authority of the head of household, or 'patriarch.'

36 This is a loose usage, which illustrates some of the problems involved in the concept of the Asiatic mode of production; there were in fact several different 'Oriental' forms of property which had little in common other than their divergence from the forms characteristic of Western European feudalism or modern capitalistic society.

37 'Istoriia drevnego mira vo "Vsemirnoi istorii" podgotovliamoi Akademiei Nauk SSSR,' *VDI* (1952), no. 1, p. 8.

38 E.M. Shtaerman, 'K voprosu o krest'ianstve v zapadnykh provintsiiakh Rimskoi imperii,' *VDI* (1952), no. 2, pp. 100–21; Shtaerman, 'Problema padeniia rabovladel'cheskogo stroia,' *VDI* (1953), no. 2, pp. 51–79; A.P. Kazhdan, 'O nekotorykh spornykh voprosakh istorii stanovleniia feodal'nykh otnosheii v Rimskoi imperii,' *VDI* (1953), no, 3, pp. 77–106; A.R. Korsunskii, 'O polozhenii rabov, vol'nootpushchennikov i kolonov v

zapadnykh provintsiiakh Rimskoi imperii v IV–V vekakh,'
VDI (1954), no. 2, pp. 47–69; S.I. Kovalev, 'K voprosu o
kharaktere sotsial'nogo perevorota III–V vv. Zapadnoi
Rimskoi imperii,' *VDI* (1954), no. 3, pp. 33–44; M.Ia.
Siuziumov, 'K voprosu o protsesakh feodalizatsii v
Rimskoi imperii,' *VDI* (1955), no, 1, pp. 51–67; S.L.
Utchenko and E.M. Shtaerman, 'O nekotorykh voproskah
istorii rabstva,' *VDI* (1960), no. 4, pp. 9–21. I am omitting
from the list of articles cited here, and from the analysis in
the text, material on Hellenistic Asia Minor and on
Ptolemaic Egypt, which raises rather different issues and
depends on a different source base. The material on Egypt
of the Pharaonic period proper will be included (according
to the accepted, though not entirely rational, procedure)
under the Near East. The discussion on social relations in
the Western Roman Empire was summarized and
commented on, at various points in its development, in the
following editorials: 'Problema padeniia
rabovladel'cheskogo stroia (k itogam diskussii),' *VDI*
(1956), no, 1, pp. 3–13; 'Za glubokoe ovladenie
teoreticheskim naslediia Lenina,' *VDI* (1957), no, 1, pp.
3–16.

39 E.M. Shtaerman, 'Problema padeniia rabovladel'cheskogo
stroia,' pp. 54–55.

40 Kovalev, 'K voprosu o kharaktere,' p. 44.

41 I will list here only the most significant of the materials on
the Ancient Near East, omitting those on ancient India for
reasons similar to those for which the materials on
Ptolemaic Egypt and Hellenistic Asia Minor were omitted
from note 38. A.I. Tiumenev, 'O znachenii termina 'kal' v
drevneshumerskom iazyke,' *VDI* (1946), no. 2, pp. 10–20;
V.V. Struve, 'Problemy istorii Drevnego Vostoke v
sovetskoi istoriografii,' *VDI* (1947), no. 2, pp. 17–41; A.I.
Tiumenev, 'Khoziaistvennye personal khrama Bau v
Lagashe vremeni Urukaginy,' *VDI* (1948), no. 1; V.V.
Struve, 'Naemnyi trud i sel'skaia obshchina v Iuzhnom
Mezhdurech'e,' *VDI* (1948), no, 2, pp. 13–33; A.I.
Tiumenev, 'K voprosu o naemnom trude v tsarskom
khoziaistve vremeni III dinastii Ura,' *VDI* (1950), no. 1,
pp. 48–52; I.M. D'iakonov, 'Reformy Urukaginy v
Lagashe,' *VDI* (1951), No. 1, pp. 14–32; E.V. Cherezov,
'Sotsial'noe polozhenie *mrt* v khramovom khoziaistve
Drevnego Tsarstva,' *VDI* (1951), no. 2, pp. 40–6; I.M.

Lur'e, 'Drevneegipetskie terminy *meret* i *khentiushe* vo vremeni Drevnego tsarstva,' *VDI* (1951), no. 4, pp. 73–80; I.M. D'iakinov, 'Gosudarstvennyi stroi drevneishego Shumera,' *VDI* (1952), no. 2, pp. 13–37; E.V. Cherozov, 'K voprosu o znachenii drevneegipetskikh terminov *merit* i *khentiushe* vo vremeni Drevnego Tsarstva,' *VDI* (1952), no. 2; A.I. Tiumenev, 'Proizvoditeli material'nykh blag v tsarskom khoziastve vremeni III dinasti Ura,' *VDI* (1954), no. 1; I.M. D'iakonov, 'Kuplia-prodazha zemli v drevneishem Shumere i vopros o shumerskoi obshchiny,' *VDI* (1955), no. 4, pp. 10–40; A.I. Tiumenev, 'Perednyi Vostok i antichnost,' *Voprosy istorii* (1957), no. 6, pp. 50–70, and no. 9, pp. 40–46; N.B. Iankovskaia, 'Zemlevladenie bol'shesemeinykh domovykh obshchin v klinopisnykh istochnikakh,' *VDI* (1959), no. 1, pp. 35–51; I.A. Stuchevskii, 'O spetsificheskikh formakh rabstva v drevnem Egipte v epokhe Novogo tsarstva,' *VDI* (1960), no. 1. In separate categories, we should note the editorial 'K obsuzhdeniiu prolemy istorii proizvoditelei material'nykh blag v drevnemmire,' *VDI* (1962), no. 3, pp. 3–11, which discusses some issues relating to the status of the immediate producers in Pharaonic Egypt, as these issues stood at the time of publication; and a review of W.L. Westerman's *Slave Systems of Greek and Roman Antiquity* by A.R. Korsunskii, V.I. Kuzishchin, Ia. A. Lentsman and I.S. Sventitskaia (*VDI* (1958), no. 4, pp. 136–58) which raises points relevant to the discussion both of the classical social order proper and of that of the ancient Near East.

42 A.I. Tiumenev, 'Perednyi Vostok i antichnost' (cited hereinafter as *PVA*; for full data, see note 41).

43 Originally published in *VDI* (1963), no. 3; English translation first published in *SA&A* vol. 2 (1963), no. 2, pp. 32–46; reprinted in S.P. Dunn and E. Dunn (eds), *Introduction to Soviet Ethnography* (Berkeley, 1974), pp. 519–48. For the record of the discussion on this paper, see 'Diskussia po probleme rodovoi i sel'skoi obshchiny na Drevnem Vostoke' (*VDI* (1963), no. 1), translated in *SA&A*, vol. 2 (1965), no. 4, pp. 61–5 and vol. 3 (1965), no. 1, pp. 37–53.

44 'Comparison of the characteristics of the basic and superstructural phenomena in Egypt and the Fertile

Crescent on the one hand and of the countries of classical
culture on the other, shows clearly, in our opinion, that in
the history of the ancient and Eastern classical
slaveholding societies we have, not two successive stages
of the development of slaveholding (as is supposed by the
prevailing theory in Soviet scholarship), but two different
types of slaveholding society. The special character of the
base – which was precisely the broadest exploitation, along
with slave labour proper, of the labour of the local
population as well – conditioned not only the distinct
character of the superstructural phenomena (the despotic
character of the political superstructure, the prevalence of
religious doctrines in the field of ideology), but also an
entirely different path of development distinct from that of
the classical world. Whereas the system of slavery in pure
form which existed in the classical countries led their
entire economic and social life into a blind alley from
which it was necessary to seek an escape in various
directions, in the East in the countries of riverine culture,
the development proceeded in the direction of a gradual
softening of the forms of exploitation – from exploitation
not differing in any way from slavery, to a milder form of
transference of particular land parcels to dependent
tenants. This evolution was observed both in the Fertile
Crescent and in Egypt' (Tiumenev, *PVA*, Part II, pp.
55–6). This passage is of particular interest from the point
of view of traditional, formal Marxism, because, assuming
that slaveholding represented one social order and
feudalism another, one would expect that a revolution, or
at least a very sharp and painful experience for the society
as a whole, would have to intervene between them. But
here Tiumenev seems to be positing a sort of mild
evolution and a general softening of the system of
exploitation, leading into a kind of quasi-serfdom.
45 I.M. D'iakonov, 'The Commune,' in *Introduction to Soviet
Ethnography*, vol. 2, pp. 519–20; emphasis in first part of
quotation added.
46 D'iakonov, 'Discussion,' *SA&A*, vol. 3 (1964), no. 1, p.
51.
47 Ibid., pp. 52–3.
48 1965, no. 1, pp. 103–10. For an English translation see
'An Exchange of Views on the Asian Mode of
Production,' *SA&A*, vol. 4 (1965), no. 2, pp. 38–46.

49   In Marx's teachings, the Asian mode of production, the
      slaveholding system, and the feudal were chronologically
      successive periods in human history. . . . The Asian
      mode of production was able to arise on the basis of the
      productive forces at the disposal of communes existing
      under conditions in which the primitive communal
      system was breaking down, but when these communes
      were unified by the major public works needed for the
      building of an irrigation network. . . .
          Thus, the ancient civilizations of the Near East and the
      eastern portion of the Mediterranean, established
      primarily by Sumer and Egypt, with their large public
      works, and then by the neighboring societies involved by
      then in the building of the world's first civilization,
      constituted the first stage in class society. In this most
      ancient class society the members of the commune *were
      exploited by the despotic authority of the rulers of Sumer
      and Egypt*, and there was also exploitation of the slaves
      whose labor was needed for digging ditches, so essential
      to the building of the irrigation system. The slaves were
      the joint property of the communes, and as the
      large-scale agricultural economy developed further, the
      number of slaves increased and the proportion of slave
      labor became greater, as is evident from the Sumerian
      economic-report documents, starting with the 24th
      century BCE (V.V. Struve, 'The Concept of the "Asian
      Mode of Production," ' *SA&A*, vol. 4, no. 2, pp. 44–5
      (*emphasis added*)).

      The reader will note that the underlined phrase implies
      disagreement with D'iakonov's position, just cited, to the
      effect that commune-members as such were not exploited.
      It remains unclear whether D'iakonov and Struve are
      talking about the same period of time, but in any case
      Struve (unlike D'iakonov) does not connect the
      exploitation of commune-members with the disintegration
      of the commune itself.
50   See particularly L.S. Vasil'ev and I.A. Stuchevskii, 'Tri
      modeli vozniknoveniia i evoliutsii dokapitalisticheskikh
      obshchestv,' *VI* (1966), no. 5. Translated in *The Soviet
      Review*, vol. 8, (1967), no. 3, pp. 26–39. A substantial
      selection from the early stage of the discussion (five
      separate items) was translated in *Soviet Studies in History*,

vol. 4, (1966), no. 4, pp. 3–45. Part of this material is
purely informational in character, but its importance
should not be underestimated, since it acquainted Soviet
readers for the first time since the Second World War with
the history of the earlier discussions, and to some extent
with the political circumstances surrounding them. In
addition to the material already cited, see the articles by
Iu. I. Semenov and G.A. Melikishvili translated in S.P.
Dunn and E. Dunn (eds), *Introduction to Soviet
Ethnography*, vol. 2, and also the following: O.A.
Afanas'ev, 'Obsuchdenie v Institute istorii AN SSR
problemy aziatskogo sposoba proizvodstva,' *SE* (1965),
no. 6, pp. 122–5; Iu. M. Garushiants, 'Ob aziatskom
sposobe proizvodstva,' *VI* (1966), no. 2, pp. 83–100; M.A.
Vitkin and N.B. Ter-Akopian, 'Po stranitsam zhurnala
"La Pensée," ' *Voprosy filosofii* (1965), no. 3, pp. 172–6
(translated in *SA&A*, vol. 4, no. 2, pp. 46–51).

51 The principal difficulty encountered by historians of
ancient Eastern societies is the contradiction between
the model that envisages these societies as slave-holding,
and the factual data confirming that the predominant
bulk of the population was the stratum not of slaves but
of petty producers exploited through a system of taxes
and duties to the state. It was the exploitation precisely
of this stratum that provided the bulk of the surplus
product.

Students of the early Middle Ages encounter a similar
contradiction between the model and the facts. In the
majority of early medieval states considered to be
feudal, the individual most commonly encountered was
also the petty producer with an independent farm, and
the large-scale landed property and large-scale
landholding typical of feudalism were absent. Many
historians found a way out of this difficult situation by
classifying all tribute and land taxes as feudal rent, and
their recipient (the state or some other corporate body of
the ruling class) as owner of the land. But Marxist theory
holds that the nature of property defines the essence of
exploitation and the dependence of the direct producers,
and not *vice versa*. Taxes and feudal rent may be
demonstrated to be identical only if one has first proved
that the property on the basis of which they are exacted

is feudal in nature. It is utterly false to classify all rights of a government to dispose of the land of its subjects as manifestations of feudal property in the land (L.V. Danilova, 'A Discussion on an Important Problem,' *Soviet Studies in History*, vol. 4 (1966), no. 4, p. 5; first published in *Voprosy filosofii* (1965), no. 12, pp. 149–56; translation slightly changed to correct a grammatical error).

The same author later refined and elaborated this position considerably: see L.V. Danilova, 'Controversial Problems in the Theory of Precapitalist Societies,' *SA&A*, vol. 9 (1971), no. 4, pp. 269–328 (originally published in *Problemy istorii dokapitalisticheskikh obshchestv*, Moscow, 1968). However, the important aspect of the article quoted here is the date, which specified the time when the three-stage model ceased to be authoritative. It should also be noted that Danilova's position implicitly contradicts the thesis according to which identity between rent and taxes was a major characteristic of the Asiatic mode of production – or at least it sharply limits the applicability of this thesis; if one wishes to maintain it further, one must then show the existence of some third form of property characteristic of antagonistic societies, other than feudal or capitalist property.

52 I list here the more significant of the publications making up the recent discussion (that is, since 1965) on the Asiatic mode of production. The list will be divided into books (including collections) and individual articles. It will be roughly chronological within each category.

See especially *Obshchee i osobennoe v istoricheskom razvitii stran Vostoka*, ed G.F. Kim *et al.*, Moscow, 1966; K.K. Zel'in and M.K. Trofimova, *Formy zavisimosti v vostochnom Sredizemnomor'e v ellinisticheskii period*, Moscow, 1969; E.V. Blavatskaia, E.S. Golubtsova, and A.I. Pavlovskaia, *Rabstvo v ellinisticheskikh gosudarstvakh V III–I vv. do n.e.*, Moscow, 1969; Iu. V. Kachanovskii, *Rabovladenia, feodalizm ili aziatskii sposob proizvodstva?*, Moscow, 1971, pp. 72–3; *Problemy dokapitalisticheskikh obshchestv v stranakh Vostoka*, ed. G.F. Kim, Moscow, 1971, p. 160. Among the articles, see: I.M. D'iakonov, 'Osnovnye cherty ekonomiki v monarkhiiakh drevnei Zapadnoi Azii,' *NAA* (1966), no.

1, pp. 44–58; V.M. Masson, 'Stanovlenie ranneklassovogo obshchestva na drenem Vostoka,' *VI* (1967), no. 5, pp. 82–94; Iu. M. Garushiants, 'Ob aziatskom sposobe proizvodstva,' *VI* (1966), no. 2, pp. 83–100; G.A. Melikishvili, 'Nekotorye aspekty voprosa o sotsial'no-ekonomicheskonstroe drevnykh blizhnevostochnykh obshchestv,' *VDI* (1975), no. 2, pp. 18–44 (for English translation see 'Some Aspects of the Question of the Socio-Economic Structure of Ancient Near Eastern Societies,' *SA&A* vol. 17, (1978), no. 1, pp. 25–72); same author, 'The Character of the Socio-Economic Structure in the Ancient East,' *SA&A* vol. 15 (1976–7), nos 2–3, pp. 29–49, originally published in NAA (1972), no. 4, pp. 53–64; G.F. Il'in 'Rabstvo i drevnii Vostok,' *NAA* (1973), no. 4, pp. 51–70; I.M. D'iakonov, 'Slaves, Helots, and Serfs in Early Antiquity,' *SA&A*, vol. 15, no. 2–3, pp. 50–102 (first published in *VDI* (1973), no. 4, pp. 3–29). Korostovtsev, 'O poniatii "Drevnii Vostok",' *VDI* (1970), no. 1, pp. 3–17; V.N. Nikoforov, 'Logika diskussii i logika v diskussii (O ranneklassovykh obshchestvakh),' *VI* (1968), no. 2, pp. 113–26; Iu. I. Semenov, 'The Theory of Socio-economic Systems and the Process of World History,' *SA&A*, vol. 16 (1977), no. 1, pp. 3–26 (first published in *NAA* (1970), no. 5, pp. 82–95).

For a perceptive critique of the discussion on the Asiatic mode of production from a slightly different angle see the article by Jan Pečirka: 'Die sowjetischen Diskussionen über die asiatische Produktionsweise und über die Sklavenhalterformation,' *Eirene* (1964), no. 3, pp. 147–69; 'Von der asiatische Produktionsweise zu einer marxistischen Analyse der frühen Klassengesellschaften (Randbemerkugen zur gegenwärtigen Diskussionen in der UdSSR),' *Eirene* (1967), no. 6, pp. 141–75. In these articles, Professor Pečirka has attempted – and to some degree accomplished – the same task which I set myself in the present monograph.

53 That is to say, acting explicitly or implicitly in the interest of a particular group or class on whom they directly or indirectly depend.
54 Kim *et al.*, eds, op. cit., pp. 3–4.
55 I use this term to designate generically what I take to be the revisionist forms of Marxism or quasi-Marxism

espoused not only by Marx but also by such Third World
leaders and thinkers as Julius Nyerere and Frantz Fanon.
In my usage here, the words 'exceptionalist' and
'revisionist' carry no pejorative connotation, since I hold
(in contrast to what is apparently current Soviet official
doctrine) that strict classical Marxism is inapplicable to the
Third World – which is to say preindustrial conditions.

56 Ibid., p. 28.

57 'Essentially the present discussion up to now is properly
speaking not a discussion of the theory of the Asiatic mode
of production, but a discussion of the contemporary
concepts of the slaveholding system in antiquity.' Ibid., p.
33.

58   The petty producer can be fully exploited only in a
feudal way, since both slavery and capitalism destroy
petty production. But if ancient societies were founded
on the petty producer, who could only be fully exploited
through feudal exploitation, then consequently the
ancient societies were either undeveloped . . . or
developed feudal societies (ibid., p. 46).

Other Soviet classical historians such as E.M. Shtaerman,
have pointed out what appears to be the fact – that the
large-scale use of slaves to produce goods for the market,
as in the Roman *latifundia* of the very late Republic and
early Empire, represented an exceptional situation in the
classical world, and therefore should not be made the basis
of a special order, without additional evidence.

59 See G.F. Kim *et al.*, eds, *Problemy dokapitalisticheskikh
obshchestv v stranakh Vostoka*, Moscow, Nauka
Publishing House, Main Editorial Office for Oriental
Literature, 1971. An editorial note on the verso of the title
page states that the editors regard this book as a kind of
continuation of the earlier volume edited by Kim, but that
all the contributors to the present volume are essentially
agreed that the traditional five-step sequence of social
orders is the best reflection of what actually happened in
history. We shall see in a moment that this is something of
an oversimplification of the views of at least some of the
contributors.

60 Here, as in some other places, I use the term 'Marxian'
(contrasted with Marxist) to designate the doctrines
developed by Marx and Engels themselves, as over against

later developments in the traditions, influenced by data, intellectual currents and historical events unknown to them.

61 There is no question that the conception of Marx and Engels is entirely definite; it can be traced from the moment of its birth to that final form which it received in Engels' work, *The Origin of the Family* . . . the conception as to the economic order of the precapitalist East may in fact change on the basis of recent data unknown to Marx in his time and to the investigators on whose works he based himself. It does sometimes happen that one has to return from the conclusions which seem the latest word to the first hypothesis – from the printed work to the first draft. But if what we have before us is just such a case – that is, if the proponents of the Asiatic mode of production prove finally to be in the right – not even this would give them the right to identify their viewpoint with that of Marx and Engels (let alone with Lenin's).

 If some people now dispute the Asiatic mode of production, they of course are not referring in essence to the views of Marx and Engels. What Marx and Engels in the 1850s contributed on their own to the concept of 'Eastern' society – namely the search for a material basis for the history of the East – is certainly correct, and is not quarreled with by any Marxist. The argument essentially turns on whether the concrete picture of Asiatic society drawn by historical scholarship in the first half of the 19th century is correct, or whether the picture drawn by late 19th century scholars (which Marx and Engels were also able to take account of) is correct (ibid., p. 38).

62 Ibid., pp. 87–8.
63 I.M. D'iakonov, 'Slaves, Helots, and Serfs in Early Antiquity,' *SA&A*, vol. 15 (1976–7), nos 2 and 3, pp. 50–102; this was originally published in *VDI* (1973), no. 4.
64 G.A. Melikishvili, 'Some Aspects of the Question of the Socio-Economic Structure of Ancient Near Eastern Societies.'
65 D'iakonov introduces at this point an important and far-reaching qualification: full property in the modern sense did not as a rule exist in the ancient world, simply because the productive cycle at that time depended to an

extreme degree on factors of chance – that is, natural conditions, weather (or access to irrigation water), wars, and the like – and therefore any farming operation other than that of the state itself could exist only by close cooperation with others like it. Although D'iakonov does not make the following point here, this qualification places a severe limitation on the validity of the close parallel between ancient (particularly Greco-Roman) society and that of the modern capitalist world, which was made many years ago by M.I. Rostovtzeff, and which has been echoed in recent years by some Soviet scholars such as Shtaerman and Melikishvili.

66 Kim *et al.*, eds, *Problemy*, pp. 132–3.
67 Ibid., pp. 134–5.
68 Ibid., p. 137.
69 Ibid., p. 139.
70 See Kobishchanov's contribution to the 1965 discussion, quoted and discussed earlier; see also, for that matter, the statements by the editorialist for *Vestnik drevnei istorii* as far back as 1947.
71 D'iakonov, 'Slaves, Helots, and Serfs,' p. 81.
72 See, for example, the critical articles published in *Saeculum*, vol. 11 (1961). While it is true that this publication antedates much of the Soviet discussion dealt with in the present monograph, nevertheless sufficient material was already available in 1961 to indicate that the situation was not as simple or one-sided as the contributors to this volume wished to make out.
73 M.I. Finley, *Ancient Slavery and Modern Ideology*, London, Chatto & Windus, 1980, p. 70.
74 Ibid., p. 164.
75 'Die Anfänge der antiken Gesellschaftsformation in Griechenland und das Problem der sogennannten Asiatischen Produktionsweise,' *Jahrbuch für Wirtschaftsgesgeschichte* (1971), pp. 29–48.
76 Finley, *Ancient Slavery and Modern Ideology*, p. 164: 'his use of the term "social formation" is significantly different from that of Anderson,' Anderson, at the point cited, says:

Throughout this text, the term 'social formation' will generally be preferred to that of 'society'. In Marxist usage, the purport of the concept of social formation is precisely to underline the plurality and heterogeneity of possible modes of production within any given historical and social totality. Uncritical repetition of the term 'society', conversely, all too often conveys the assumption of an inherent unity of economy, polity or culture within a historical ensemble, when in fact this simple unity and identity does not exist. Social formations, unless specified otherwise [sic] are thus here always combinations of different modes of production, organized under the dominance of one of them (Perry Anderson, *Passages from Antiquity to Feudalism*, NLB Press, London, 1974, footnote on p. 22).

77 See K.K. Zel'in, 'Principles of Morphological Classification of Forms of Dependence,' *SA&A*, vol. 6 (1968), no. 4, pp. 3–24. Originally published in *VDI* (1967), no. 2, pp. 3–20. This article was reprinted, with some significant additions and omissions, in Zel'in and Trofimova, op. cit. (see note 52). The analysis which follows is based mainly on the later version.

78 Zel'in, 'Principles of Morphological Classification,' pp. 4–5.

79 The reference here is apparently to V.V. Struve, 'Obshchestvennyi stroi ellinisticheskogo Egipta,' *VI* (1962), no. 2, pp. 67–95.

80 Zel'in and Trofimova, *Formy zavisimosti*, pp. 37–8.

81 Ibid., p. 41. As we will see in a moment, there are other places where slaves (in the juridical sense) are not necessarily deprived of the means of production, which introduces yet another complicating factor.

82 Zel'in, 'Principles of Morphological Classification,' pp. 10–11 (emphasis added).

83 Zel'in and Trofimova, op. cit., pp. 63–4.

84 G.A. Melikishvili, 'Nekotorye aspekty voprosa o sotsial'no-ekonomicheskomstroe drevnykh blizhnevostochnykh obshchestv.' See also Melikishvili, 'The Character of the Socioeconomic Structure in the Ancient East (A Preliminary Classification of Class Societies by Stage and Type),' *SA&A* vol. 15, (1976–7), nos 2–3, pp. 29–49; originally published in *NAA* (1972), no. 4, pp. 53–64. Here Melikishvili, as it were, draws the conclusion from his argument on the nature of ancient Near Eastern society, proposing what is in essence an

extreme simplification of the traditional Marxist sequence
of social orders which would leave only three – primitive
communism, class society, and advanced communism. This
proposal, like Semenov's even more radical ideas along
the same lines, will not be discussed here, since it is as yet
too early to predict their outcome, and in any case they do
not relate directly to the controversy on the Asiatic mode
of production.

85 See Shtaerman, 'The Society of Classical Antiquity: The
Modernization of History and of Historical Analogies,'
Soviet Sociology, vol. 10 (1971), no. 2, pp. 107–62. This
was originally published in *Problemy istorii
dokapitalisticheskikh obshchestv*, vol. 1 (1968).

86 The counterposition of these sectors to each other was
hardly so tangible or sharp in the ancient East. After all,
in relation to the all-powerful state, people living on
lands which are declared in the sources to belong to the
king or the temple . . . and on other lands, were in fact
little different from each other. They all paid taxes in
kind, all bore the same obligations in terms of labor,
military service, etc., and the economic burden placed on
the so-called free commune member apparently was
often no less severe than that of producers living on
'royal lands' (Melikishvili, 'Nekotorye aspekty,' p. 30).

87 See A.I. Neuskyhin, 'Dofeodal'nyi period kak
perekhodnaia stadiia razvitiia ot rodoplemennogo stroia k
rannefeodal'nomu (na materiale istorii zapadnoi Evropy
rannego srednevekov'ia),' *VI* (1967), no. 1, pp. 75–87.

88 I have been told by recent Soviet emigrés that certain
particular scholars – A.Ia. Gurevich is the most notable
example – have been deprived in recent years of the
opportunity to teach and publish their views, and that
others have been subjected to minor forms of harassment.
It seems significant, however, that the participants in the
discussion on the ancient Near Eastern social order, and
related topics such as the essential characteristics of
slaveholding, are not among them, nor do they include
those such as Iu. I. Semenov, who have made some of the
most radical proposals in regard to the Marxist theory of
history in general. I was also told by the late David
Zil'berman that the publication of 1968 of *Problemy istorii
dokapitalisticheskikh obshchestv* (which included articles

expressing a wide range of highly heterodox views) was an
aberration reflecting a particular combination of
circumstances at the time, and would have been quite
impossible either earlier or later. This may well be true:
Zil'berman's tragic death in England during the summer of
1977 prevented my pursuing the matter further with him.
However, it should be noted that there has been no
general silencing of the contributors to this collection, and
it is referred to with some frequency in the subsequent
literature – by no means always negatively.

89 Iurii Ostrovitianov and A. Sterbalova, 'The Social
    "Genotype" of the East and the Prospects of National
    States [Part I],' *SA&A*, vol. 16 (1977), no. 1, pp. 31–2
    ('Sotsial'nyi "genotip" vostoka i perspektivy
    natsional'nykh gosudarstv,' *Novyi mir* (1972), no. 12, pp.
    208–20). Since this article carries no footnotes, I am
    unable to place precisely the origin of the quotation from
    Engels which is incorporated here, but I believe that it
    comes from *Anti-Dühring*.

90 Ibid., p. 36. The emphasis in the second part of this
    quotation is my own.

91 *Rabovladenia, feodalizm ili aziatskii sposob proizvodstva?*,
    Moscow, Nauka Publishing House, Main Editorial Office
    for Oriental Literature, 1971.

92 This is the 'classical' Aziatchik position as it was held
    during the 1920s. See note 36 of part one of this
    monograph. To my knowledge, no Soviet scholar now
    maintains this and in fact Kachanovskii gives no
    present-day reference for it.

93 See Semenov, 'The Problem of the Socio-Economic Order
    of the Ancient East,' in S.P. Dunn and E. Dunn, eds,
    Introduction to Soviet Ethnography, vol. II, pp. 575–604
    (originally published in *NAA* (1965), no. 4); and
    Garushiants, 'Ob aziatskom sposobe proizvodstva,' *VI*
    (1966), no, 2, pp. 83–100.

94 Kachanovskii, op. cit., pp. 7, 8, 9, 12.

95 Ibid., p. 77.

96 Ibid., pp. 155–6. Emphasis mine.

97 Ibid., pp. 167–8.

98 Ibid., p. 171.

99 Iu. V. Kachanovskii, 'O poniatiiakh "rabstvo" i
    "feodalizm",' *VI* (1967), no. 6, pp. 123–34.

100 That is to say that presumably the property in this case

does not include the persons of the immediate producers, as it does under slaveholding. By this reasoning, it is an interesting question what Kachanovskii would make of late Russian serfdom, between 1762 and 1860.

101 The text by D'iakonov referred to here is apparently 'Problemy sobstvennosti. O strukture obshchestva Blizhnego Vostoka do serediny II tys. do n. e.,' *VDI* (1967), no. 4 (for English translation, see *SS* vol. 7 (1968–9), no. 3, pp. 9–32). In his later work, analyzed earlier in the present monograph, D'iakonov refined this typology somewhat.

102 At this point, Kachanovskii contrasts D'iakonov's view with that of Tiumenev, who held that the communal peasants were exploited.

103 Kachanovskii, *Rabovladenie, feodalizm*, pp. 222–3.

104 M.A. Korostovtsev, 'Rabovladel'cheskaia formatsiia v svete istoricheskogo materializma,' in *Problemy sotsial'no-ekonomicheskikh formatsii: istoriko-tipologicheskie issledovaniia*, Moscow, 1975, pp. 78–89.